Cross Media Marketing 101
The concise guide to surviving in the C-suite

By James D. Michelson

Schooner Press

Cross Media Marketing 101
By James D. Michelson

Copyright © 2011 by Schooner Press. All rights reserved.

Printed in the United States of America.
First Printing: January 2011

www.schoonerpress.com

THIS EDITION IS AVAILABLE FOR BULK SALES. PLEASE CONTACT SCHOONER PRESS IN THE UNITED STATES AT:

sales@schoonerpress.com • www.schoonerpress.com

Submissions for Publication

Schooner Press accepts unsolicited submissions from authors without representation. Submit cover letter, synopsis, and entire text to editor@schoonerpress.com. Simultaneous submissions are not accepted. Submitted materials will not be returned.

Library of Congress Cataloging-in-Publication Data

Michelson, James D
Cross Media Marketing 101 / James D. Michelson

ISBN-13: 978-0615435756
ISBN-10: 0615435750

Table of Contents

Contents

iv

Why Cross Media 1

Why Cross Media

First, the bad news. There is no silver bullet technology that will generate leads and provide staggering return on investment. Each of the various cross media channels can provide trackable and measurable results when used properly, but they need to be part of an overall marketing and sales plan that capitalizes on the strengths of each channel. A weak economy, downward price pressure, the requirement to focus on quarterly or monthly results, and other challenges have taken a very real toll on sales and marketing leaders. Because of these challenges, the average tenure of a Chief Marketing Officer is less than two years and an executive in the sales organization gets less than nineteen months. Perhaps survival is a greater challenge than success. In order to beat these odds, a better set of tools must be used to justify marketing spend and to define results in an objective way.

Business leaders in the board room are demanding that an increasing portion of the marketing budget be dedicated to web and social media outlets. Survey after survey, year after year, shows the shift from traditional marketing channels to new media. Print, newspapers, and other old line advertisers continue to suffer. The chart shows research from 2010.

The good news is that there are simple and cost effective ways to combine traditional marketing techniques with emerging technologies to capitalize on this trend. An easy to execute cross media strategy can provide measurable results which will allow sales and marketing executives to make informed decisions on

What Marketing Tactics Does Your Company Plan to Spend More or Less on in 2010?

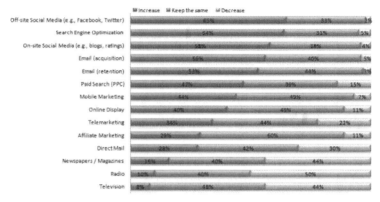

Source: Econsultancy and ExactTarget, Marketing Budgets 2010: Effectivenss, Measurement and Allocation Survey, January 2010, N=265

where to focus company efforts and resources. By proving effectiveness and return on investment, a marketing or sales leader can demonstrate a plan for moving the bar incrementally and creating long term value.

Every few years there seems to be a great idea that gets co-opted as a catch phrase by bad marketers looking to make an average product or service somehow remarkable. One recent example of this phenomenon was the word extreme. After the success of a youth oriented series of sporting events, everything from business forms, mini-golf and snack chips were referred to as extreme, xtreme, or XTREME !!!! Extreme business forms? Seriously?

3

The latest word to be drafted into the pantheon of hucksters looking to peddle one particular solution or another is "cross media."

What Cross Media Marketing is: A method of using multiple channels to provide a unified marketing message that features a call to action on all of the channels employed to drive respondents to a single data collection point in order to start a two-way conversation.

What Cross Media Marketing is NOT: Anything else.

Marketers have been issuing the same message on multiple channels since the inception of mass marketing. Coordinated TV, radio, and print ads are nothing new. What makes a campaign become cross media or cross channel is how the responses are funneled into a single data collection point, either systematically or manually, to generate a dialogue with the prospect. The creation of a two-way dialogue is the key feature. Marketers need to gather information from their clients and use that information to generate the follow on communications – regardless of channel. Any channel or medium can be employed. Anything else is just advertising.

Despite fact that media has splintered and traditional tactics are increasingly less effective, most large advertisers continue to pursue the same strategies which were widely used in 1985. That may not seem like all that long ago to many of us, but remember, the internet wasn't in common use for another ten years!

Many large agencies excel at creating national brand campaigns but falter terribly when they try to engage in personalized cross media marketing. One major agency chief executive told me recently that although they understand the value of new technologies, if they can make a million dollars on a TV campaign, why bother with $15,000 on an email program for small customers. The fact of the matter remains that staffing levels are down and unlikely to rebound in the short term, even if marketing spend rebounds to pre-recession levels. So, where do corporate marketers and business leaders turn for support?

The gap caused by the combined lack of interest and vision in the agency world has led to an opening for commercial printers and small specialty marketers to support beleaguered marketing and sales executives. These companies are transitioning into Marketing Service Providers (MSPs) along the fringes of the big agency world. They are fielding inquiries from clients with agencies of record who cannot or will not provide cost effective cross media services.

Where does this leave the sales and marketing executive at the end of Web 2.0? They must understand the strengths and weakness of the various media channels and the service providers that offer them. That is not to suggest that every CMO be an expert at everything from search engine optimization to television production, but they need to fundamentally understand how each channel is employed and whether it should be handled in-house or outsourced.

GETTING BURNED

As commercial printers and small design houses realize that they need to adjust their offering to remain competitive in the market, they have embraced the idea of becoming marketing service providers (MSPs). Many only acquired the tools and not the marketing savvy to execute complex cross media campaigns. The result is that many marketing and sales executives have been burned by new media campaigns that were expensive to launch and difficult to execute. That may leave the marketer wary of turning to specialty firms or consultants, either brick and mortar or web based, to help execute the strategy. The most common reason cited as to why these programs are not employed is that the bandwidth to manage multiple providers and coordinate the results is beyond the firm's capability. When staff reductions and hiring freezes are added to the mix, the task of integrating new media becomes daunting.

Many sales and marketing executives have struggled with new media technologies that were incorrectly executed. Hardware manufacturers set unrealistic expectations that service providers, who took the manufacturers at their word before they had real world experience, could never meet. Outrageous claims were originally made by some solution vendors and trade organizations such as the Direct Marketing Association (DMA) about the response rates typically generated with new and even traditional techniques. In fact, they still continue to make such claims.

Cross media channels and technologies were sold by marketing service providers desperate to believe the hype in order to boost flagging revenue and recoup their investment in new hardware and software capabilities. The unreasonable expectations that were set, when combined with the inexperience of the providers, caused far too many viable projects to fail. Many did so in spectacular fashion. Not only did these parties overpromise and under deliver, but they also used the "fantastic" response rates to charge exorbitant prices. There is no wonder why many traditional organizations have not made the switch to more advanced techniques. With a little common sense and caution, the time has come to move forward.

Take Away

A study conducted by Spencer Stuart shows the life span of a CMO has dropped to less than two years. In order to survive, sales and marketing leaders must coordinate brand across sales channels, control brand message, employ measurement tools and accurately calculate ROI.

✔ In 2007 the average lifespan of a CMO was 26.8 months

✔ In 2008 that figure had dropped to 23.6 months and by 2009 it had slipped to 23.2 months

✔ Only 37% currently have more than 3 years of tenure

To do well, a leader must focus limited resources on what works best and have measurable proof that justify the selections made.

7

With increased demands from business leaders for accountability, decreasing budgets, and fewer staff hours, the pressure to perform and succeed every time is growing. It is critical to understand the application of these tools in the overall marketing plan and to select in-house personnel or vendors that have the appropriate skillset to execute them in a cost effective and efficient manner.

Regardless of the position held in sales, marketing, or any senior management position, a general understanding of the new media market and how these channels can work together is critical. The ability to challenge service providers and to reasonably assess the value of each channel will help assure that the decision making process can systematically measure relative effectiveness. Not only will this process maximize return on investment by allowing marketers to focus spend on the most effective channels, it will also improve marketing and sales leader's longevity.

Take Away

The early failures of many cross media projects should not discourage executives from taking a fresh look at techniques that can drive response rate and ROI when judiciously applied. Starting with inexpensive and easy to implement cross media processes, organizations can begin to build a robust data collection and marketing platform at low risk and without large budgets.

Traditional Media Channels 2

Traditional Media Channels

The pundits who have sounded the death knell for traditional media are overstating the case. Although the last decade has been hard for newspapers, magazines, television and traditional print, they are still powerful forces in marketing and sales. The growth of digital and social media may have stolen the buzz from these channels, but count on them reversing their declines and holding steady in the coming years.

According to Forrester Research, by 2014 an estimated 21% of all marketing spend will be made on new media with a value of $55 Billion.

This means that 79% of marketing dollars with a value of $207 Billion will still be directed at traditional media channels. It is imperative to leverage this spend to maximize return by adding new media response mechanisms.

A popular series on cable for the last several years (the fact that it is popular and on cable should tell us something immediately about traditional media channels) is Mad Men. The series revolves around a fictitious advertising agency. The social concerns of the characters may be biased to the times and a Hollywood social and political agenda, but the firm that they work for operates in pretty much the same way as many agencies today.

These firms pitch a branding concept and design advertising, packaging, and broadcast messaging to disseminate the new idea. They make money by collecting a markup on the ad space they broker. This process may be good for the agency and the media outlets, but how valuable is it to the Chief Marketing Officer or Vice President of Sales? The last thing that a network or magazine wants their advertisers to be able to measure is the true effectiveness of the ad space in selling products purchased on a spot by spot basis.

For the owner of the advertising real estate or the air space, the circulation is the magic number to sell. For the advertiser, this number should be irrelevant. Bigger may be better, but the number of listeners or readers who respond should be the key metric. A media buy is only worth the leads it generates to those of us responsible for results. In today's budgetary environment, a subjective gauge of the value of marketing dollars spent is a sure way to decrease job security. It may be true that broad advertising builds brand awareness, generates buzz, keeps the brand at top of mind, etc, but the C-Suite needs tangible results to pass on to the board and stockholders. Many firms that have virtually universal brand recognition spend far too much on brand awareness.

Conventional wisdom says that branding is a key element of the marketing plan and so expenditures that cannot be measured are a necessary evil. Do not except this tenant as truth. Every channel can be measured by adding mechanisms to capture data and create a two-way conversation. Any argument to the contrary is part of a sales pitch designed to overcome objections.

This is not to say that any particular channel is a poor marketing choice. The burden rests on the advertiser to measure results and select those channels that deliver the best return for their particular product or service. The most effective channels may or may not be part of the current marketing mix. There is only one way to find out - test, measure, and repeat. The chapters that follow will explore how to execute such a strategy without big budgets and agency or IT department support.

The mechanics of executing marketing campaigns using the traditional channels have changed very little since 1950. Advertising has traditionally relied, and to some degree still does, solely on frequency and reach to be effective. John Wannamaker, the illustrious Philadelphia retailer, coined the common adage that half of all marketing dollars are wasted, but there is no way to know which half. Known as a competent and frugal operator in Philadelphia circles, Mr. Wannamaker would certainly have used every means possible to track what his marketing spend was doing.

The internet has given marketers the opportunity to provide customers what they perceive to be an anonymous channel to research a product or service in a manner that they control. Traditional media channels have historically operated in a vacuum where the most coordination that could be managed was a similar fit, feel, and sound across the various media. There was no easy way to gather response metrics and in the event metrics were gathered, to consolidate and analyze the data. A summary of the traditional channels follows.

TELEVISION, RADIO, AND PRINT ADVERTISEMENTS

Most senior marketers still remember clearly when there were only five or six television stations in most major metropolitan areas. ABC, CBS, NBC, PBS, and one or two local UHF market providers were it. PBS did not yet offer advertising. The airwaves were priced out of the range of most small to medium sized businesses unless manufacturer co-op funds were available.

When cable came on the scene in the mid-eighties it featured dozens of channels which initially struggled to attract advertisers. The most popular cable networks were ad free and other niche stations like ESPN aired high school lacrosse games and MTV actually broadcast music videos. Neither channel started with any paid advertising. These channels developed into major media franchises over time and were in the vanguard of the dilution of all forms of media.

Small to mid-sized business could compete with the national brands in print using newspapers and regional trade magazines. After the rise of CNN, popular online news aggregators such as the Drudge Report, and news blogs for every vertical, newspapers have suffered huge losses in both circulation and advertising revenue. At the time of this writing, major cities such as Boston are in danger of losing their sole local newspaper. Other cities have already lost their print news outlet or have watched the content become available online only.

Small marketing budgets usually focused on local media such as billboards, radio, buses, and small local papers. Services could

13

always rely on the yellow pages. Consumers were easier to target using just a few channels. Challenges arose with the ever-increasing fragmentation of media. Cable now has hundreds of channels and most of them are ad revenue based. Specialization helps some marketers with targeted audiences not only on a channel level, but also on a show by show basis. For the provider of general goods and services, this is a major challenge as the audience continues to fragment.

There are certain advertisers that greatly benefit from content specific stations. For example, home improvement chains and equipment makers are a perfect match for Home and Garden Television (HGTV) and these firms can reach a very targeted audience based on the highly specific content of the programming. Garden tool makers advertise during garden shows and window companies buy airtime during remodeling shows.

In other media, newspaper circulation continues to plummet and magazines are more specialized and numerous than ever. This radical change in the landscape is why understanding and engaging in cross media has become so critical. The customers and still out there, but they are spread further apart than ever.

DIRECT MAIL

There is still no substitute for placing the firm's marketing message directly in the hands of the desired individual. Direct mail has a reputation for being expensive and without the use of modern targeting techniques that reputation had a basis in truth. Like any process, it is often the methodology and execution of the channel, and not the methodology itself, that is at fault for poor results. Lacking any better way to select recipients, many marketers relied (and still do) on "spray and pray" or throwing "stuff" up against the wall to see what sticks. This is neither an efficient nor cost effective way to reach customers. Blasting messages often does real harm to the brand as uninterested recipients often receive materials they do not want. For the record, I do not now, nor have I ever had, a time share. There is a compelling case on why direct mail is still king and will be examined in depth in a later chapter.

STREET TEAMS & EVENT MARKETING

National brands passing out free samples or placing signage at the stadium remains a powerful way to directly reach large numbers of consumers. The variety of possibilities for direct interaction with a target audience is almost limitless. The cost of sponsoring many events or their venues has dropped in recent years, but these are still major outlays that run in the hundreds of thousands if not millions of dollars. Prior to the implementation of cross media marketing there was little or no way to ascertain if the sponsorship of a particular event generated sales or reached the desired target audience. These kinds of expenditures lay at the heart of the "half the marketing budget is wasted" dilemma. To be effective and provide a measurable return, experiential marketing must utilize cross media channels.

15

CALL CENTERS

The utilization of call centers, either staffed internally or outsourced to a third party vendor, has been common for many years. Recent efforts to shift customer sales and service efforts abroad, first to India and then to Asia seem to be on the wane as quality assurance and customer satisfaction losses overcame any financial gains of utilizing foreign centers. The ability to append demographic data to phone numbers that are identified and then matched against national consumer databases is also not new. Traditionally, this data was used for fulfillment purposes only or was lost in a silo and never passed on to sales or marketing. The broad application of internet technology on call centers has changed their potential in the modern marketing mix despite the implementation of a National Do Not Call list.

DEATH OF THE PRESS RELEASE & TRADITIONAL MARKETING

Press Releases were written and distributed first by snail mail and then eventually by email. Web sites such as PRWeb were developed that accepted submissions from public relations firms and marketers for distribution across a variety of online channels. For a time, an expenditure of several hundred dollars would result in tens of thousands of hits to the content and the website it referred to. The effectiveness of this strategy has dissipated over time. But the need to disseminate this information has increased.

I was probably the last tech executive to buy a smart phone. I was also skeptical that social media would ever be a legitimate business tool, but the shift away from traditional marketing practices became quite clear to me in 2008. In 2007 our firm used a press release to announce the launch of a new product and generated a 1200% increase in web traffic for the month. The same process and investment in early 2009 resulted in no statistically significant change in traffic.

Is the press release dead? Maybe not, but the method of distribution of the content has radically changed. If anyone is going to read that release or if media outlet is going to pick the story up, the story had better make it onto a popular blog or content specific site. The rules keep changing. What worked online last year probably won't next year. The challenge for marketing and sales leaders will be to keep ahead of the curve. That last sentence sounds a lot like "Buy Low, Sell High" advice. Now let's examine how to do it.

Getting Started *3*

Getting Started

What can the executive do to assure that they are getting the most out of their marketing and sales dollars? The answer is easier than may be apparent. First, insist that each channel employed in the marketing plan utilizes multiple response mechanisms that start two-way conversations with the customer or prospect. The era of the marketing push is over. Second, assure that brand, offer, and message consistency is kept across all media and distribution channels. Third, assure that data from multiple channels is not created and subsequently stored in silos, especially if those silos reside under the control of another department or vendor.

When marketers think of cross media, they generally start with a traditional brick and mortar business and consider how to incorporate email and web into the marketing mix. The need to get into cross media marketing is as important for web businesses as is it is for everyone else. After making an online purchase, I subsequently received a direct mail catalog from eBags.com. I had not responded to any of their electronic offers and the mail piece was likely triggered by my lack of action. According to the United States Postal Service, consumers are far more likely to make online purchases if they have received a catalog or direct marketing solicitation. Similarly, zappos.com, a darling of the e-tailing world, can frequently be seen advertising in various print magazines as can Google, Bing and Yahoo.

What is Cross Media Marketing?

Cross media marketing is not a technology. A quick search on the internet will provide dozens of "cross media solutions" that each have a different meaning according to the products offered. This marketing concept is also more than using multiple channels to push the same advertising message. An offer that appears on an email and direct mail piece at the same time does not qualify as cross media.

Take Away

Cross media works with any marketing mix. The more exposure the product or service has across more marketing channels, the larger the audience. The chance that the right channel will be utilized increases exponentially. Adding simple data collection and opt-in processes will maximize the value of the various channels and offer measurable insight into those that perform.

Cross media marketing is the implementation of a comprehensive plan for the creation of two-way conversations with prospects and customers. It is a unified strategy that shares brand identity and focus across marketing channels. It is a method to collect and analyze data in one place gathered from multiple sources. There is no one way to implement a cross media strategy. A detailed description of how each advertising and sales channel can be incorporated into a plan follows.

The common thread is to utilize the web to gather both leads and actionable intelligence from every touch. From point of sale and call centers to billboards and radio spots, the web can be leveraged as the low cost service destination to start a dialogue with consumers. This strategy is not designed to replace any marketing method. It is designed to leverage all channels employed and provide cost-effective, easy-to-use measurement and tracking tools and to collect prospect data in one location that can be easily accessed by staff outside of the IT department.

There is, as mentioned earlier, no silver bullet that will create a cross media marketing platform to drive explosive growth despite common claims on the web to the contrary. In fact, no comprehensive platform is required at all. While technologies may be useful in the implementation of a cross media marketing plan, a substantial technology investment is not required. The channels and strategies that will be discussed can be executed by any size firm without an increase in staff, change to the marketing mix, or reallocation of the budget.

In every step of the sales cycle from basic research, data collection, caparisons of features, benefits and price-to-product reviews, both business and consumer buyers are turning to the web for research. Our data shows that for every direct action taken (such as a phone call or email) four to seven additional reviews are made of content online. A second touch to this group of indirect responders can yield spectacular results at very low risk. Marketing and sales executives need to assure their content appears in online research. Cross media one to one (or 1:1) marketing is the ideal platform for presenting complex sales material to both consumers and businesses.

Take Away

For every direct action taken (such as a phone call or email) four to seven additional reviews of content are made online. A second touch to this group of indirect responders can yield spectacular results at very low risk.

Key benefits of cross media marketing include convenient ways for marketers to:

▸ Drive traffic to the selected content

- Identify prospects that have visited the website and target those customers for follow-up

- Determine the key demographics of the best clients and ways to target similar potential prospects

- Coordinate marketing efforts across all media channels

- Track prospects that visit a web page but take no action to build a "warm" lead list

- Build brand awareness and capture current sales opportunities

- Increase brand loyalty and maintain residuals longer

- Create opt-in marketing & newsletter information programs

- Receive detailed reports on program effectiveness

- Test and focus efforts on most profitable messages

Women Over 55 and Facebook

The number of US women over age 55 using Facebook grew by 175.3% between September 2008 and February 1, 2009. This makes mature females one of the fastest growing demographic groups on the social network according to usage statistics released by the independent blog Inside Facebook. The number of men over age 55 also grew dramatically during the same period and was up 137.8%. Facebook's international audience has also continued to grow. In particular, the network has rapidly gained popularity with people over the age of 45, growing by more than 165% among both men and women.

Cross media marketing for savvy web users is not just for kids and twenty-somethings. Every age group is actively involved in social media and the web.

The Two-Way Conversation

Executives that will excel in the next five years will implement data collection and analysis processes at every contact point with the customer. The technology used to execute this part of a well designed cross media marketing strategy does not need to be complicated. The capability can be acquired with varying levels of complexity on a monthly subscription basis from various vendors for less than $50 per month. The more automated the processes across channels, the more expensive the solutions become. As long as the data collected is being funneled into one location, even manually, then the basic requirement is met.

If certain advertising or direct marketing programs are institutionalized and cannot be altered (as is frequently the case at many firms), these programs can still be leveraged for cross media marketing. Adding inexpensive new or additional collection and response mechanisms will help boost response and provide metrics. An offer-specific landing page that is unique to each channel, or even to individual advertisements is the most cost effective way to immediately implement this strategy regardless of the marketing mix. These cross media mechanisms are indispensable additions to marketing campaigns that will help executives justify the spending decisions they make.

The true power of cross media marketing is to create opportunities for two-way conversation with potential and current clients. By driving visitors to the web and personalized landing pages, marketing and sales professionals can create a cost effective and automatic mechanism for collecting data and executing follow up communications based on customer actions.

Active Data Collection

By asking specific and direct questions of identified web visitors, marketers can gather data and save that information for use in targeted marketing efforts. Opt-in marketing functionality allows firms to capture contact information on interested consumers. Personalized web pages are a perfect tool to use for data collection because the web page already has the visitors contact information and all the consumers have to do is click "Opt-In".

Take Away

By actively and passively collecting data on visitors, marketers can make touch points more relevant to the recipient. The more relevant the communication, the better the results.

Generic URLs & Personalized URLs

Generic URLs (GURLs) or Static URLs are used when the recipient is not known in advance on channels such as radio, television, or print advertising in newspapers, magazines and trade publications. The content is tailored specifically toward the advertisement and tracking can measure the number of leads generated from a particular channel or individual advertisement.

Personalized URLs (PURLs)

Personalized URLs are used when the recipient of a marketing message is known in advanced on such channels as direct mail or email. A typical call to action would be:

Visit your personalized web page for special offers: www.vip.mycompany.com/JoeClient

Even if the web visitor does not take any additional action, the marketer will know on a name by name basis who visited the web, thus capturing a warm lead list.

This functionality makes the opt-in process painless for the customer and the data entered is not mistyped, increasing accuracy. Once the customer has visited the website, the next step is to open an ongoing relationship. Make sure to keep information and brand in front of the customer by offering materials such as a newsletters, personalized direct mail, or email bulletins. The content of these materials must be relevant and timely to assure the continuing willingness of the target audience to remain receptive to the outbound communications. At each touch, solicit input from the recipient.

After identifying the visitor from a variety of consumer databases or proprietary data sources, the process loads a personalized web page with further information on the offer which reinforces the call to action. The page can appear to be part the main corporate web site. Each web page can feature an automatically populated form for opt-in marketing based on the data look up. Real time personalization is a variable data marketing process that transitions prospects from traditional media to a personalized web experience. The process allows marketers to capture the identity of the visitor using minimal input to append a demographic and psychographic profile. The process does not require a login or account to be created. Using this information, each recipient is served personalized web content in real time based on the persona developed from their input. The web site can capture each visit and deliver an instant email sales alert.

Passive Data Collection

By tracking what actions a web visitor takes during a session, a good indicator of their areas of interest is created. Marketers can use that information to tailor future touches. The identification of visitors is therefore of paramount importance. For example, if four offers are highlighted in large buttons and a visitor selects two of them to investigate, the follow-on communication could feature the selections made. For consumer products, the follow-up could be a coupon, unique offer, or a rebate. Business to business campaigns could offer literature or a case study.

Message, Customer, Time and Channel

The basics of getting noticed in the new media market have not changed. Marketers still need to get the right message to the right customer at the right time. The right channel, on a customer by customer basis, has been added to the mix.

The Right Message

New online and printing technologies allow for the cost-effective deployment of multiple versions of the same marketing. Each piece can easily be tailored to the selected demographics of the individual recipient. A detailed analysis allows the customer to be targeted with the right message based on a persona.

The Right Customer

An effective variable data campaign begins with a data analysis of current and potential customers. The result of the review is a highly targeted list of recipients for individually customized direct mail campaigns. Too many firms, especially major business to business and business to consumer sales organizations skip this step with disastrous results.

The Right Time

The data analysis is combined with the individual product or service's sales cycle to create a direct marketing campaign. Proper repetition is the key. Variable data printing and email can make it cost-effective to target both existing customers and prospects with custom mail pieces, email, web pages, and opt-in marketing.

29

The Right Channel

As part of the two-way conversation initiated with prospects and customers, it is crucial to determine their contact preferences as part of the survey and opt-in process. By asking how customers wish to be contacted, it is possible to continue conversation in a manner most likely to keep the prospect engaged over time. This is not to say that the indicated communication method should be the only way the prospect receives touches from the firm, only that the specified channel(s) should be given preference.

The type of organization that is engaged in this methodology does not change the process itself. Brick and mortar retailers, business to business distributors, service companies, and even web firms need to follow this process. It is unwise for merchants and suppliers to assume that customers who order online only wish to be contacted by email. It is very possible that the type of communication desired by the customer will vary based on the content. The only way to be sure is to ask.

FOUR STEPS TO CROSS MEDIA MARKETING

There are four steps that must be accomplished to create an effective cross media campaign, regardless of marketing mix employed.

Step 1: Developing Personas

While every customer is different, they have demographic similarities that make them alike, especially in relation to the product or service being offered. The exact same item can be targeted to different groups by changing the channel and advertising message.

Sample Lead Generation Campaign with Personas

Take the example of a cruise ship operator that has one product with a single itinerary that needs to be sold across many demographics. A quick analysis of the business reveals that there are four personas which can be targeted; Singles, Young Couples, Married with kids, and Seniors. The content of each channel can be targeted to the demographic based on the profile of the persona created. On mass marketing channels targeting parents, advertisements can feature children's activities for family time by the pool and child care that allows for romance. Singles are targeted with adventure activities and the night club, and so on for each segment.

This kind of targeting is not a new concept. What is new is the call to action in the marketing piece that drives the prospect to the web using a unique web address. Use an alternate site such as www.cruisewithkids.com for the web call to action instead of www.cruiseline.com/family where the "/family" tends to be dropped. Additionally, another department such as IT usually needs to be involved to get the page added to the corporate site. The unique web address drives the visitor to a specific page that

31

is tracked to the particular advertisement, measures response on that particular channel, and also offers the visitor an opt-in form without the need to click through to another site or page to take the call to action. Once the visitor is identified by opt-in, that persona can be targeted with follow on communications based on the channel preference they have indicated.

The usual objection that comes from most marketers at this point is "I have had forms on my website for years and almost nobody uses them." True enough, although several simple but significant changes to what has always been done are made. First, the opt-in form as a call to action will be prominently featured on a channel specific landing page, not buried in the company website. Second, a web component will be prominently featured on every touch, not just a few selected campaigns.

If the cruise line in this example is going to pay for television, radio, and magazine ads they will be purchasing millions of impressions. What if just 0.1% of 20,000,000 impressions goes to the page and opts in to the offer? There are 20,000 warm leads ready for a second touch, narrowing a virtually infinite universe of prospects to a manageable number to contact directly.

What was the change required to make these opt-ins possible? A content specific landing page was added to capture web traffic that was already occurring. How many ads do not already have a web address on them? Give the target audience a reason to take action now. The sample campaign shown leverages existing marketing spend to capture additional leads.

Sample Campaign Results – Cruise Line

Channel	Impressions	Opt-In %	Identified Leads
Radio	4,000,000	0.1%	4,000
Television	12,000,000	0.1%	12,000
Magazine	800,000	0.1%	800
Pay Per Click	40,000	0.1%	40
Total	*16,840,000*		*16,840*

A quick glance of the chart shows that an insignificant response rate can generate many new leads. Even small firms with limited touch points can capitalize on this technique to passively generate leads off of the current marketing mix without making any fundamental changes to the plan or budget.

Step 2: Determine Assets

This book assumes that sales and marketing managers and other business executives have limited access to data from their organization. If this is not the case, so much the better, but in reality there are two typical scenarios that most firms fall into. One common setup in large firms sees the responsible manager with only sporadic access to summary data or periodic data dumps from another department. The political capital required to access data in a customized fashion and on demand is far too high to be practical. The data may exist, but the brand manager for a particular product may not get the support he needs. The second scenario is typical in small and mid-sized firms where the organization does not have the IT and data support required. In many small firms, these functions may be outsourced on a part time basis. In short, just because information is available in a server somewhere, it does not mean the marketer can get access to it. The first step, therefore, is to take a survey of the data that is available. Consider all the following silos of data that may exist:

▸ Customer files from CRM and sales reps

▸ Warranty card information

▸ Opt-in lists and product inquiries

▸ Purchase histories

▸ Social media followers (blogs, Twitter, etc.)

▸ Lists from email and newsletter opt-ins

▸ Web site accounts

▸ Special event mailing lists

▸ Acquired data

▸ Partner, vendor or distributor files

This list is by no means exhaustive. There are likely additional sources that come to mind from your specific organization.

The second part of this process is to assure that the collaterals portray a consistent brand message. It is critical to control materials being created outside of marketing by field personnel or branch offices to assure that they match the fit, feel, messaging, and data collection of the corporate effort. The amount of data lost in the field as it sits in silos can be staggering. CRM initiatives were designed to alleviate this problem, but their use is problematic. According to common research, upwards of half of these implementations fail. They have not worked in the past because there is too much effort to execute the data input and collection on the part of line personnel. This situation may improve with near universal access to high speed internet connections but it will remain a process that requires staff input.

The following CRM and IT project failure rates were reported by ZD Net in August 2009 and are typical.

Year	Source	Failure Rate
2001	Gartner Group	50%
2002	Butler Group	70%
2003	Selling Power, SCO Forum	69%
2004	AMR Research	18%
2005	AMR Research	31%
2006	AMR Research	29%
2007	Economist Intelligence Unit	56%
2009	Forrester Research	47%

Step 3: Leverage Existing Efforts

Legacy marketing efforts and programs that command fixed portions of the budget may occur for a variety of reasons. Even if these expenditures can not be eliminated or scaled back to meet the needs of a changing marketing environment, additional collection mechanisms can still be added to engage customers in the required two-way conversation. By utilizing the various cross media tools, the case can eventually be made for the future of the program in question. Only in the face of hard data will it possible to accurately judge if the expenditures are contributing appropriately to the bottom line. As previously discussed, add generic landing pages and other cross media mechanisms to start a meaningful two-way conversation.

Step 4: Build New Channels

To prepare a cross media marketing campaign, follow these production steps to assure a smooth process. Run through the following five steps whether you are using a software as a service or free cross media channels when preparing your campaign to minimize the risk of failure.

1. Define the Goal

Every campaign has different needs and expectations. First prioritize the requirements. Draw up the functional requirements based on the needs of the project. It is amazing how often this step is skipped at firms of all sizes. The result is projects that do not meet the needs of the organization and waste time, effort and assets.

2. Develop a Clear Plan of Action

The planning phase is the most crucial element of a project. First, develop a realistic development plan based on the functionality requirements. Decide what to implement by prioritizing those items that will begin to produce immediate results.

It is important to ensure that everything implemented is fully scalable and will upgrade to the next level without excessive complications.

3. Build a Strong Foundation

The original functional blueprint will serve as documentation for the proposed campaign, site and web applications. This documentation also will serve as a record for any future modifications on the code, allowing other programmers and web designers to make modifications and enhancements as necessary. Formal planning and functional blueprints make sure that the project is well documented. Ensure this process continues through additions and modifications.

4. Put the Plan to Action

Create websites and applications using the current top of the line development software or services that can grow with you. This allows for rapid and scalable development over time. For websites, the pages are first constructed in a general form. Menus, headings, basic text and functions are added allowing a test drive of the new site. A functional web site will emerge as work continues. Through feedback and testing, fine tune the operation of the site.

5. Keep Current

Ongoing updates and marketing can be provided after the campaign has been deployed. Critical operations such as monitoring traffic and calculating return on investment should be completed regularly. A reporting system that puts the success of the month's activity into relative context is used to evaluate performance. Changes can be made as necessary. Make sure this capability resides within your area of responsibility and control to minimize long term operational difficulties.

Marketers need an easy and systemic way to touch customers in multiple media channels and to track the responses received. As discussed, the key to making cross media marketing campaigns effective is not simply placing the same message on the different media. The ability to collect and analyze data on responders in a systematic way is critical. A principal goal must be to determine customer contact preferences and touch them accordingly. Here's how.

DETERMINING CUSTOMER PREFERENCES & CONTENT

A crucial part of the two-way conversation with customers is determining the prospect's or client's contact preferences. There are three steps to accomplish this task.

Capture Visitors

The first step in the process is to implement a means to capture prospects that are responding to the advertising message but are not making contact or taking the call to action. Marketers should drive prospects to the web and discover the visitor's identity by employing Personalized URLs or Real Time Personalization (RTP). The easiest way to capture web visitors has been the use of Personalized URLs (PURLs) which use variable data printing to target known recipients with relevant content both in print and once they arrive at a customized landing page. This process can be cost prohibitive for cold solicitations with low or moderate price points. Since it is not always known in advance who is going to see the message, the use of generic landing pages can provide a mechanism to start the two-way conversation.

Static and broadcast media can drive prospects to a landing page that utilizes Real Time Personalization to create a demographic profile and serve personalized content on the fly using only their name and zip code. By adding real time personalization to the campaign's landing page and phone responses, marketers can create an actionable database of responders. Opt-in or contact forms on line are not enough. Data from VDP Web® shows that only 1 in 15 respondents to a solicitation online will opt-in by filling in a form. The key is to capture visitors even if they do not call or fill out a form. These concepts are examined in more detail in the next chapter.

Group the Responders

The data collected by real time personalization includes not only what information the visitor reviewed, but also their demo-graphic traits from national consumer databases. Without addi-tional expense, this list can easily be segmented into groups. Advertisers will not only know who responded to their ads, but also what traits they have in common. These include age, estimated income, presence of children, credit worthiness and more. This intelligence allows marketers to craft the product message specifically for the prospect by creating personas and presenting relevant content.

Select Touch Points & Execute Campaign

Once respondents have been identified and segmented, the next step is to determine what message to send. Different campaigns can be run based on a variety of goals.

▶ Automatic Follow-Up: Target prospects that responded to the advertisement but took no further action with a series of solicitations to turn them into customers.

▶ Cross-Sell & Up-Sell: Prospects that purchased can receive follow on pieces to market additional products and services

▶ Life Cycle Management: Thank you notes, re-order reminders, referral programs, and special events can be coordinated around the sales cycle.

CONTENT MANAGEMENT

After data collection, the most daunting task for most firms is managing a host of print and web collaterals. Consider the years of marketing materials made by long departed employees, contractors and defunct or acquired agencies. There are obsolete design files, lost originals, inconsistent naming conventions and the data may be held in multiple servers and storage locations. It is easy to appreciate the complexity of content management for companies of all sizes. If the firm is doing business in more than one country or in a nation with multiple dialects, the content problem becomes exponentially more difficult. The prospect of getting and keeping all this material under control can be daunting. Content management promises to consume more of the marketer's time as channels continue to multiply. This section takes a brief look at the key items that marketing leaders need to consider.

Planning

The first step in content management is to get all marketing materials into one place from all divisions, branches, product lines or departments. This is a critical first step for CMO's seeking to get a handle on larger organizations. For marketers without the ability or political capital to influence other departments, collect as much content as you can in a centralized location. As part of your consolidation efforts, make sure that all staff and vendors that will do work on your marketing collaterals have a solid understanding and follow the guidelines and rules for the brand. Every size firm should have a Brand Manual. Create a new one or update the existing manual and distribute it to any person or organization producing content.

Brand Manuals and Standards

If the firm does not already have one, consider creating a brand and style manual. This document specifies colors, fonts, design elements, logo usage, and scaling (size) for both print and web. Organizations with an agency of record or those that have employed a professional design house often have a document or at least the makings of one. This manual establishes rules that

41

act as a guide for designers and programmers so that consistency is maintained in all marketing materials across the organization and vendors.

Sample Brand Manual

The brand manual will help keep you out of trouble with the legal department as well. It can specify trademark requirements, disclaimers, and all the other legal mumbo-jumbo that copywriters, designers and programmers need to include in the design.

Advanced Content Management

Although a comprehensive guide to implementation of advanced content management is beyond the scope of this book (and beyond most marketers for that matter) a general understanding of the concepts is adequate. Most firms rely on many creation, delivery and fulfillment platforms to process their information. These can vary widely in companies within the same vertical. Any particular vendor or service that a marketer may wish to use may not be compatible with the firm's files and formats. This can dramatically limit the options available for fulfillment of such functions as order taking and payment processing.

XML

Extensible Markup Language (XML) is a simple text format used to structure and pass data in a consistent way. XML is a set of rules for encoding documents in machine-readable form for use on the internet and in print. Although the design of XML focuses on documents, it is widely used for the representation of many data types. XML documents are text data and they do not rely on any particular application. Not only can the data be exported to a variety of applications, it can also be stored for long periods of time without becoming obsolete. An XML document can be transformed into a different structure or format, such as HTML for the web or CSV for databases. With XML, each individual piece of information is "marked up" with a tag that attaches meaning to the information and allows it to be displayed in various ways. Many application programming interfaces (APIs) have been developed to process XML data. Numerous XML-based languages have been developed, including RSS, Atom, SOAP, and XHTML. XML-based formats have become the default for most office productivity tools including those from Microsoft and Apple.

DITA

The Darwin Information Typing Architecture (DITA) is an XML-based architecture for authoring, producing, and delivering technical information. It consists of a set of design principles for creating "information-typed" modules at a topic level and for using that content in various delivery platforms such as online help and product portals on the Web. DITA has features that serve to organize and integrate information. Topics can be reused and is made into new information types which can then be used to produce a variety of content. For example, a brochure, a web page, and an article are all potential materials created from a topic. DITA builds on industry standard tags and can be delployed with common XML tools. The XML processing model is supported by a growing number of software vendors. DITA topics can be processed by a variety of tools ranging from shareware to custom tailored products on almost any platform.

The evolving world of marketing communication is more complex and dynamic than ever before. A content management process can help firms:

▸ Meet compliance and standardization needs

▸ Reuse content easily across multiple channels in the marketing mix

▸ Lower localization costs by delivering XML and DITA content

▸ Reduce time to market by repurposing existing content

▸ Improve the ease of publishing to multiple formats (including print, PDF, XML, and HTML) and devices (including mobile phones, eBook readers, and tablets) from a single data source

Specialized Data Formats

Traditionally, firms have relied on specific user interfaces that cannot interact with other systems to take orders, process payments, or conduct other business. A standard way of describing data and fields allows any application to process the transaction. Auto Dealer Format XML and Open Order XML are two standards that represent the possibilities of content management. By using a defined set of fields, these standards for auto dealers and shopping carts allow different applications to seamlessly interact. Business leaders can leverage the market presence of other platforms or channels to drive sales and decrease the complexity of fulfillment without investing in custom implementations for every channel.

THE BOTTOM LINE

Cross media marketing campaigns are a cost-effective and powerful tool for building and expanding a client database, increasing brand awareness, staying in front of customers, entering the sale cycle at the right time, capturing current sales opportunities, and managing customer life cycles. By using the data collected from real time personalization, soft leads, surveys, and opt-in marketing, highly targeted campaigns can be developed that will increase response rates and improve ROI.

KEYS TO SUCCESS

The critical elements to the success of any cross media campaign can be quickly summarized.

▶ Systematically collect data on customers and prospects in one location, keep the data current and segment those leads and clients into personas. Understand your data file before you communicate.

▶ Make every communication an opportunity to begin a two-way conversation. Never waste a touch point.

▶ Maintain brand consistency across all channels and funnel leads into a single data collection mechanism.

▶ Make every touch timely and relevant with easy opt-ins. Start a two-way conversation by asking questions, adding PURLs, using links to landing pages with content relevant to the message, and utilizing segmentation and personas.

Take Away

✔ By adding content specific landing pages with opt-in forms to the current marketing mix, firms can capture an actionable list of interested prospects without adding budget.

✔ Real Time Personalization can capture visitor demographics with minimal input and serve variable content on the fly.

✔ Respondents can then be grouped based on demographics and response metrics which are used to serve targeted messages that speak directly to customer needs and personal characteristics.

✔ Automatic touches to clients can take the burden off the sales team and allow staff to focus on the best leads only engaging them after multiple touches.

✔ Make every communication an opportunity to start a two-way conversation. Never waste a touch point.

Cross Media Channels Part I *4*

Cross Media Channels Part I

There is no one best way to execute a cross media campaign. The various channels available must be evaluated for their potential effectiveness and return. They must be rigorously tested as they are incorporated in a firm's existing marketing mix. Any marketing channel, from small giveaways to multi-million dollar television campaigns, can incorporate these tactics to provide tracking, accountability, and ultimately boost ROI. Entire books have been written about each of these channels. The purpose of this discussion is to show how cross media marketing techniques can be incorporated into each.

The primary goal of cross media marketing is to create an actionable database of warm leads that can be targeted with follow on touches to maintain and advance the sales cycle. For every prospect that directly engages from a marketing effort by executing the call to action, four to seven will visit the web to investigate the offer further. When a marketing effort is launched, firms will note a corresponding spike in web traffic. In the vast majority of cases, these web hits have been wasted sales opportunities because there has been no mechanism to passively capture the visitors' identity or provide an easy method to opt-in without navigating through the corporate site.

Throughout this chapter, various marketing channels will be presented. There will be two distinct measures provided for each channel. Cost will be scored from one to three dollar signs. The price breaks for cost are arbitrary figures and are meant to reflect the degree of difficulty in getting new expenditures approved by a single sales or marketing decision maker.

$	Less than $1,000
$ $	$1,000 - $10,000
$ $ $	$10,000 plus

The degree of difficulty to execute a particular channel item are defined as Easy, Moderate, Difficult, and Very Difficult. This again is a subjective measure and is based primarily on two factors. The first consideration is the level of expertise required to execute a particular channel and the second is the time and effort, including assistance from other departments or company assets, required to bring a project to completion.

Easy projects should take less than twenty man hours to initiate and require no assistance from departments outside either sales or marketing. Moderate projects take twenty to eighty man hours of time and require minimal outside assistance or only a moderate amount of help from other departments. Difficult projects require long periods of time or are difficult to execute and usually require outside assistance. Very difficult projects may be expensive, time consuming, require extensive interdepartmental assistance, or any combination of these issues.

STATIC LANDING PAGES

 ($) [**Easy**]

The traditional method of utilizing the web for offline marketing efforts is to print or say the company web address in the copy. Visitors are driven either to the company home page (where they are expected to navigate around to find the relevant content) or to a content page. Marketers have occasionally added an offer code to the web address such as www.myfirm.com/offer in an attempt to use a special page on the website to present specific content. This technique may drive web traffic, but it does not provide a means to identify and directly contact the visitor. Additionally, split testing has shown that prospects frequently truncate or forget the "/offer." The solution is to create a special web address for the campaign by either acquiring a new address such as myfirmoffers.com or using a DNS record such as www. offer.myfirm.com. Altering the company web site in order to accommodate the new page may be difficult to execute with the IT department or the outside contractor or agency that manages the site. So an entirely new web address controlled by marketing may be the easiest solution.

The landing page created for the offer content should have the following characteristics.

▸ Call to action above the fold

▸ Easy to identify next step

▸ Opt-in form

This technique can be used on any channel to help identify and capture visitor data from the spike in web traffic.

Sample cross media landing page

The landing page provides the opportunity not only to serve offer specific content, but to also conduct brief surveys that allow for data collection. The generic URL for the landing page can appear on any advertising medium either printed or broadcast. By including this functionality on every single marketing interaction, it is possible to create an automated lead generation mechanism that leverages the sunk costs of other marketing.

The new content can be a single page or an entire website. See the case study in Appendix A for a sample. There is very little opportunity cost associated with this process regardless of the marketing mix. This is an especially powerful tool for marketing service providers such as traditional agencies and commercial printers to create new revenue streams for their firms. By providing the expertise and technology to provide the data collection, these firms can become the hub around which the client's marketing strategy is executed. The leads generated can trigger automated follow up marketing activity dictated by preset business rules that the client need never touch.

The lack of both expertise and bandwidth in new media in marketing and sales departments worldwide makes it possible for various service providers to step in and provide contingency based lead generation services. This allows the service provider to gain access to marketing budgets traditionally held by other providers such as publishers and broadcast media outlets. As budgets continue their shift to new media from traditional media channels, the opportunity for service providers continues to expand. For marketers, this means support is becoming available at a better value than from full service agencies.

Savvy web marketers have long used landing pages as the entry point of their paid search marketing efforts to facilitate tracking of particular campaigns. This process assures that the prospects receive the correct content and do not need to surf through the corporate website to take action. The same tactic can be utilized with direct mail, email, and even print advertising.

The same process should be used for radio, TV, newspaper and magazine advertising to create a truly cross media marketing campaign. The expense of the advertisement is a sunk cost and most ads include a web address already. By using a landing page rather than the company home page the firm can serve the most relevant content and improve both the ease and quantity of opt-ins.

Take Away

By including content specific links to a landing page on every customer touch, a passive process of data collection will lead to an increase in opt-ins for the development of demographic information and warm lead lists that can provide automated follow up based on business rules.

PURLS & VARIABLE LANDING PAGES

($) ($) [Moderate]

Generic landing pages are used when the viewer of an advertisement is not known. For direct marketing efforts, especially by direct mail and email, Personalized URLs (PURLs) and corresponding unique web content that is segmented by individual recipient is best. Each marketing piece can contain a customized offer tailored to the recipient with variable text and graphics which features a personalized web page address. While on the site, visitors encounter an automatically populated opt–in form that asks them to take an immediate action such as to join a club, receive a newsletter, or be placed at the head of the line for special offers and programs.

The challenge with traditional campaigns featuring a web site has been the inability to know which particular recipient looked online but never made additional contact. These potential customers remain anonymous unless there is a method to capture their information. Unique URL tracking with a PURL for each prospect overcomes this challenge by capturing the propsect's visit and the actions they take on the page.

Marketers have used PURLs with varying degrees of success. Many have launched canned programs believing that the new response mechanism alone would automatically generate higher response rates. This is not the power of the PURL. The major mistakes come from the assumption that PURLs, in and of themselves, will draw responses simply because they are there. The challenge is reminiscent of the early days of 1:1 printing, when it was assumed that recipients would respond to a campaign simply because the text and graphics were database-driven. In reality, before recipients will even access their PURLs, the pitch must catch their attention. This must be followed by a sufficient incentive for the recipient to go online. This requires all of the clever marketing skills of any other campaign. As an incentive, "Hi, John. Come find out about our services" (and yes, otherwise sophisticated marketers and their customers are sending out campaigns with this pitch) is only incrementally different from that in a static mailer or print advertisement, and it will be about as effective. Too many 1:1 print providers are relying on the PURL itself—not the marketing message—to boost response rates, and then wonder why the campaign did not live up to expectations, or worse yet, the hardware manufacturer's wild promises.

Sample cross media direct mail piece with Personalized URL triggered by site visit at a race track

Top 11 Personalized URL Campaign Mistakes

✔ Going to print before the URL or DNS is pointed.

Once a marketing message has been printed or emailed, the PURL cannot be changed and if the DNS or URL changes, the firm has just spent a lot of money for nothing.

✔ When using a DNS record, not pointing the www.dns. yourfirm.com as well as dns.yourfirm.com.

People often add the www, needed or not.

✔ Relying on having time from mailing to arrival to complete web design.

According to Murphy's Law, the Post Office will always deliver the next day on bulk mail when early delivery will be a disaster.

✔ Not making the PURL the obvious call to action.

In order to capture the interest of those who take no further action, it is critical to drive prospects to the web. To succeed, the PURL must be prominently displayed on the piece.

✔ Relying only the PURL and a name to drive response.

PURLs are a great tool, but they work best when supported by other variable content such as prospect specific art & copy.

✔ Having a weak call to action.

Prospects need a reason to visit the web. Something they can not buy or easily acquire, like information, is very strong.

✔ Using too many clicks on landing page.

The K.I.S.S. principle applies to landing pages as well as the print or email design. Why take four pages to accomplish what can be done in just one?

✔ Asking too many survey questions.

Asking more than 5 or 6 questions, or using more than one web page, will cause a dramatic increase in abandonment. Ask only the questions that are crucially important.

✔ Not starting a two-way conversation.

The web landing page is ideal mechanism to gain insight into the client by having the visitor tell what they want, not just what the firm wants to know.

✔ Insufficient planning for follow up.

Make a plan now to assure that there is a system ready to go to contact the leads generated.

✔ Forcing prospects to enter an email or phone.

Unless the offer is very strong, mandating that visitors provide an email and/or phone will dramatically increase the abandonment rate. Is this information really critical and how do I know. If there is no immediate plan to utilize the phone and email, it is not critical.

TELEVISION

 Difficult

Although the cost of producing and airing television advertising has dropped in relative terms over the past several decades, it is still expensive and difficult to produce broadcast quality video. Flashy spots produced by big agencies continue to flood the broadcast airwaves but the sector is flat and likely to remain fairly steady for the foreseeable future. Ads produced on a budget come across as amateur, especially when the previous ad was professionally done with high end production values.

Even as the number of hours that Americans spend watching television continues to increase, the number of commercials they watch has not. Recorded digital television and online streaming will continue to drive this trend. Additionally, the number of channels available has skyrocketed from a few in 1980's to hundreds today, resulting in increased audience fragmentation. This is a double edged sword for marketers. Although the audience is broken down into smaller segments, it is easier than ever to target viewers by channel, show content and viewer demographics.

Major events watched live, such as sports, awards shows and the like are exceptions to that rule. The infamous Super Bowl advertisement in 2005 where the internet firm GoDaddy went "all-in" on one cheaply produced 30 second spot made the firm. The air time was over $1,000,000, but the results spoke from themselves. The shock value of the ad, which featured a scantily clad girl and a few doddering old men was made on the cheap and contrasted sharply to the slick agency ads being aired against it. It was a clever idea and the basis of a long term campaign that is still sporadically running. On the whole, consumers expect to see a high level of production values on cable and broadcast ads aired on the major channels. As will be examined later, internet video does not require this level of sophistication and may in fact be hurt by a polished and professional presentation.

Broadcast Media Case Study

A prominent sports venue in the Midwest United States spent a considerable sum on a radio and TV campaign to market ticket sales for a major annual event. The campaign targeted seven metropolitan areas within a three hour drive of the venue. Prior campaigns had featured only the main ticket number and web site. Even without a tracking mechanism, marketing executives felt certain that this campaign was driving significant sales.

In 2007 a unique phone number and web address was added to the spots to measure the result of the ad buy. The spots generated 7 calls and 24 web hits. This dismal performance did not necessarily mean that radio and television are poor sales channels. These results provide a basis on which to measure the performance of future campaigns. The time slots, stations, and copy may have been at fault. Testing of these variables can now be accurately measured against the control data to determine the value of this channel.

RADIO

 $ $ Moderate

Radio has the easiest content to produce of the traditional marketing channels. Copy writing a thirty second spot is generally less involved than most other creative. Professional production support is also reasonably and readily available in most areas. A decent spot can be created for a few hundred dollars and the production cost can often be included in the air time buy. Unlike television, there is little difference between nationally and locally produced spots.

Direct response can be a highly effective and useful tool in radio. The trick to radio is to understand reach, frequency, and audience demographics. The number, type, and duration of ads to be run depends on the goal of the campaign. An established business with a loyal clientele needs a reminder campaign with a small number of ads spread over an extended period of time. An event driven campaign requires many ads in a short period of time before the key date. Brand building and awareness requires a heavy and consistent schedule over months. It will take time and repetition to get listeners to notice and remember a new brand. Using the web to reinforce the radio copy and provide an easy opt-in mechanism can only help improve response rate at a very small incremental cost.

Radio and the Internet can be easily integrated in a coordinated marketing effort. Radio can be successfully used to drive consumers to advertised web sites and unique phone numbers.

Many radio stations have positioned their own web sites to provide advertisers cross media marketing opportunities with co-branded packages.

New York City Tea Party Event

As part of the marketing and operations for the New York City tea party event on April 15, 2009, organizers used a landing page to generate a usable database of grass roots supporters and volunteers in addition to providing an effortless registration platform. A custom designed landing page provided information and links via a static URL. The web address was broadcast for three days prior to the event on one AM radio news station, Apple 970 AM. The most powerful part of the program is that the radio spots generated hundreds of opt-ins for both the event and email, phone and SMS Text alerts regarding this event and upcoming efforts. The data was immediately available to organizers for additional fundraising and community action. Here are a few tips to keep in mind:

▸ Include a definite call to action in all copy

▸ Leverage ad specific landing pages with opt-in forms by station to generate a database of leads

▸ Make the offer dependent on a visit to the web

▸ Coordinate air time with other marketing channels

▸ Measure results via direct response to calculate ROI against other channels

LARGE FORMAT PRINT, BILL BOARDS & SIGNAGE

$ $ [Moderate]

Any large format printed media, from ads on the sides of a city bus to a bill board on the back fence of the municipal stadium or local little league park, can be easily adapted into a cross media platform. The key to gaining insight into the value of these channels to any particular advertiser lies in the call to action of the piece. Offer specific URLs, unique phone tracking, and SMS Text calls to action can generate leads from what are otherwise brand awareness efforts. Even if a very small percentage of impressions result in a web visit, call, or text opt-in, the leads that are generated are the warmest possible. Many of these ads already have some contact method on them. Like any other channel that makes a call to action, display advertising can utilize the same strategies to begin a two-way conversation with prospects. Text campaigns also work in business to business applications for trade shows, events, and any other venue where having content delivered via mobile device is important.

Typically, viewers of these advertisements are in possession of their cell phones. Consumer text to win offers can be highly effective at capturing cell phone numbers. These numbers can then be appended from consumer databases to determine the mailing address and demographics of the owner. Rates of accuracy and success on consumer lines can be very high. These contacts can then be added into the direct marketing efforts of the advertiser. Even if the consumer is not engaged over time by the text campaign, they have been identified as prospects.

First, the value of these channels for direct response has been measured and can be compared to other available expenditures. The measurement may be relative, but all other things being equal, the channel that develops the greater number of leads is most likely the better choice.

Second, a list of prospects has been generated with mailing addresses and demographics. The list can be targeted with direct marketing efforts and the data can be analyzed for patterns based on the personas of the responders to help develop relevant messaging and content.

TELEPHONE DIRECTORIES

The local phone directory is the dinosaur of the marketing world, yet it continues to be in wide use despite its exorbitant cost, massive environmental harm, and limited utility. The publishers of these books have attempted to leverage their once powerful brands into an online presence with little to no success as the search engines are the first place online consumers go. At the time of publication, one major provider was facing bankruptcy as the brand has not translated into online market share as traditional revenue falls.

If it does make sense for a firm's vertical to be in the phone book, and there are some industries where directories still generate leads, then the phone and web address listed should be unique to the advertisement so that the real value of the listing can be tracked and the return measured. The number of calls and web hits to a landing page will allow advertisers to finally assign a cost per lead to this publication. Like the large format print discussed a moment ago, adding tracking with unique numbers and landing pages will determine if the expenditure is worth the expense.

VARIABLE DATA DIRECT MAIL

 ⑤ ⑤ [Moderate]

Why Direct Mail in the Electronic Age?

According to the United States Postal Service, 97% of Americans check the mail daily and 77% at the first opportunity. Consider this scenario. When a prospect gets home or back to the office they first thing they do is check the mail. The prospect will park the car, get the mail, open the front door, pet the dog and then sort the mail over the kitchen counter. Sound familiar?

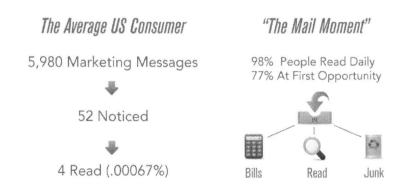

The Average US Consumer

5,980 Marketing Messages
⬇
52 Noticed
⬇
4 Read (.00067%)

"The Mail Moment"

98% People Read Daily
77% At First Opportunity

Bills   Read   Junk

We may have become a smart phone addicted business world, but how many email communications do we receive daily and how many solicitations end up in the junk folder? Additionally, how many prospects do we want to reach that we do not have their email address? The main challenge is developing an easy to use system that gets people to opt-in to email communications. Marketers need a way to cut through the clutter of 6000 marketing messages. The answer to all these issues is to put the message directly into the prospect's hands.

Sample PURL direct marketing piece

By targeting only the best prospects with relevant content, firms can dramatically reduce the environmental impact of their direct marketing effort. Rather than blanketing a city, marketers can select only those prospects that have already expressed interest in a product or service and dramatically reduce wasted mail. There is a significant environmental impact to limiting the paper, ink, electricity, and fuel required to create, print, and deliver millions of mail pieces. The best news is that the number and quality of quality leads and sales generated does not need to suffer as a result of "going green."

EMAIL

 $\$$ $\$$ Moderate

With very few exceptions, and contrary to conventional wisdom, email is not free or even less expensive than other direct marketing channels. Email campaigns do not regularly deliver staggering ROI unless a very specific set of conditions are met. Unless a firm is an online retailer or financial institution with large customer lists and detailed demographic information, developing and deploying email marketing can be as complicated and expensive as any other marketing channel. It is true that highly segmented email campaigns which target specific subsets of a customer list with specific offers can easily reach 40% to 60% response rates. If that same effort is attempted across the entire customer base the response will plummet.

According to Forrester Research, 60% of all email is still sent as "Spray and Pray" blasts. The medium may have changed, but most marketers are still firing the same generic message to the entire contact list. In order to reach response rates that exceed the norm, customers must be segmented into personas.

The example campaign featuring the cruise line showed how powerful personas can be. Certain customers will never take a cruise no matter how many times they are emailed special offers and discounts, so the need to identify interested prospects is paramount.

Most consumer and business to business emails, like many direct mail campaigns, rely on specials and discounts to generate response. This strategy is inherently flawed. The power of email is the ability to build loyalty by targeting specific individuals with relevant content based on data. Short term sales may be boosted by a discount strategy (at the expense of margin) but how does that utilize the email list to create long term value to the firm? Certain online brick and mortar retailers must perpetually offer discounts as consumers now expect them.

The first hurdle to conducting a successful email program is the collection of opt-in email addresses. The Controlling the Assault of Non-Solicited Pornography and Marketing Act of 2003 is known as the "CAN-SPAM Act." This law heavily regulates the conditions under which email marketing materials can be sent. See Appendix B for a summary of email marketing rules.

Internet and email service providers add another layer of rules and regulations in their "Terms of Service" (TOS) in order to steer clear of regulators and limit liability. These rules are becoming increasingly onerous as new rulings are made by the courts and the Federal Trade Commission (FTC). In short, marketers may not send unsolicited commercial emails. Although some rented email lists are available, every major domestic email service provider prohibits the use of these lists on their systems as part of the terms of service. Additionally, most email service providers require a discreet opt-in for each email address to be mailed above and beyond the requirements of CAN-SPAM. Marketers have two safe and accepted options available to generate an email marketing list that can be safely utilized.

The best email marketing lists will come from the combined effect of all cross media efforts. The landing page call to action on every channel should offer the opportunity for visitors to opt-in to company communications. This includes the point of purchase. If even a fraction of touches result in an opt-in, the email list will grow over time and become a powerful marketing tool. This is the secret of professional bloggers who develop contact lists and keep readers engaged with relevant content and special offers that are particularly targeted to their interests.

Tips for Generating Opt-Ins

▸ Guarantee privacy & the safety of personal data

▸ Promise not to sell, rent, or lease company email lists and contacts – the value of this type of disclaimer cannot be overstated

▸ Assure prospects that communications will be infrequent and contain relevant content – and then keep that promise

Tips for Keeping Opt-Ins

▸ Keep the promises made above

▸ Only provide infrequent, relevant, and timely information

▸ Make commercial offers a soft sell and not the primary focus of the email (unless the sender is a bulk consumer retailer and focusing on specials and discounts to drive sales)

The second method available to conduct email campaigns is to rent addresses from list owners for co-branded marketing efforts. Unlike direct mail, the sender almost never receives access to the data, only to responders. Depending on the quality and uniqueness of the list, a single use price per email sent ranges from $0.25 to $1.25 per lead. Most list owners will not allow multiple sends from the same client to help prevent the recipients from opting-out. Typical sources of these managed lists include magazine subscribers, trade organizations, client lists, not for profit membership lists, and affiliate programs such as alumni associations. Relevant content sent to a well selected list can be highly effective.

The Real Cost of Email Marketing

Email can be a critical part of any cross media marketing strategy, but it is important to understand the real cost of developing and distributing an email campaign. Email marketing is more than just sending a message from Outlook and has the same complexity as other direct marketing channels. Many seasoned executives maintain their belief that email is a practically free and universally effective way to promote their products and generate massive ROI with little effort or cost.

For firms that have an extensive opt-in email list and additional customer information to segment offers this can be true. Internet or mass market retailers and international brands that have been gathering email addresses and customer information from sales and other collection mechanisms (such as contests, information requests, etc.) can spend a few thousand dollars on design and execution to send out an effective email blast. They can achieve a very low response rate that still generates a massive return on investment.

By taking a few moments to break down the numbers, it is apparent that generating a positive return from email is not attainable for many firms. Here is how the numbers break out. The hourly rate used in the example is realistic for the actual cost of labor, but feel free to substitute your own.

For this example, these are the assumptions made:

▸ Design & Copy: 8 Hours @ $125

▸ Artwork: 2 Hours @ $125

▸ Giveaway / Discount / Offer Cost: $1000

▸ Distribution: $0.02 cents per email

▸ Response Rates: 5% and 1% purchase

Note that a 1-5% response rate requires a very targeted and engaged list combined with a compelling offer. It takes significant resources over the long term to create a successful email marketing program that can obtain conversion rates like the ones shown here.

ROI with a $5 per purchase revenue:

Quantity	Cost Total	Cost Each	5%	Net	1%	Net
1,000,000	$22,250	$0.022	50,000	$227,750	10,000	$27,750
500,000	$12,250	$0.025	25,000	$112,750	5,000	$12,750
250,000	$7,250	$0.029	12,500	$55,250	2,500	$5,250
100,000	$4,250	$0.043	5,000	$20,750	1,000	$750
50,000	$3,250	$0.065	2,500	$9,250	500	($750)
10,000	$2,450	$0.245	500	$50	100	($1,950)
2,000	$2,290	$1.145	100	($1,790)	20	($2,190)
500	$2,260	$4.520	25	($2,135)	5	($2,235)

ROI with a $50 per purchase revenue:

Quantity	Cost Total	Cost Each	5%	Net	1%	Net
1,000,000	$22,250	$0.022	50,000	$2,477,750	10,000	$477,750
500,000	$12,250	$0.025	25,000	$1,237,750	5,000	$237,750
250,000	$7,250	$0.029	12,500	$617,750	2,500	$117,750
100,000	$4,250	$0.043	5,000	$245,750	1,000	$45,750
50,000	$3,250	$0.065	2,500	$121,750	500	$21,750
10,000	$2,450	$0.245	500	$22,550	100	$2,550
2,000	$2,290	$1.145	100	$2,710	20	($1,290)
500	$2,260	$4.520	25	($1,010)	5	($2,010)

Notice that more than a 5% response rate is required in actual purchases (not just the open rate) to break even with a small prospect list. Without detailed customer information and segmentation there is little chance that such a high level of response will be achieved. If the sale is a big ticket item that requires a consultative selling process, than even a 1% response rate is highly unlikely. At 1%, the break even point comes at 100,000 emails with a $5 profit. Very few companies have that quantity of contacts to target.

 For 500 recipients the cost is $4.92 each. For 2,000 recipients, the average email size, the cost is $1.25 per piece which is more expensive than comparable variable direct mail. The recipient may get dozens of emails a day compared to four or five direct mail touches.

All other things being equal, if the value of the sale is changed to $50 then the break even at a 1% response rate still requires more than 10,000 emails to be sent.

What this example does not take into account is the cost associated with developing the email list. There are firms that claim to have double blind opt-in lists for sale and they have been used effectively for certain applications, but the response rates are nowhere near the 1% closed sale shown in this example.

List rentals from trade associations, magazines and other sources can also be advantageously used. They are usually limited to single drop campaigns and are therefore of limited utility in a long term marketing strategy. These lists can be very good for brand awareness and special events but may be cost prohibitive. Remember to add the acquisition expense in your calculations if required.

Take Away

✔ Email is not free and in quantities of less than 100,000 it can easily cost more than direct mail.

✔ The real challenge in email marketing for most firms the development of an accurate list of opted-in prospects and customers.

✔ By starting a two-way conversation on all marketing channels via content specific landing pages that give prospects a reason to opt-in, firms can steadily build contact lists over time without a change to their marketing strategy or mix.

Recent Email Additions

There is a lot of buzz now about video email. The name is a bit confusing as a video is not usually sent as part of the email. Typically, a still graphic of the video with an active link is shown in the email and that opens a browser window with a landing page that hosts the content. The new window can be a micro site, landing page, or a third party host such as YouTube.

Another recent burst of email hype has been about "trickle marketing." The allure of this methodology is apparent in an era of shrinking budgets and decreased staffing levels. In theory it sounds great. A lead is developed from any marketing channel and then an automated series of communications to reach out and touch that prospect runs without any ongoing effort. The challenges associated with developing cost effective email campaigns show that the time and expense of content creation must be factored in for the accurate determination of ROI. The conclusion was that small email lists are often as expensive to market to electronically as by any other means.

The same logic is easily applied to trickle email marketing. Unless the firm has a lead generation system that creates numerous opt-in email addresses, such as an online shopping cart that specifically asks the client to join the marketing email list, then getting enough new leads to email is the first challenge. Very few firms generate enough new leads to have a cost effective trickle marketing campaign.

Remember, just because you have a prospect's email, that does not mean you can send them an unsolicited commercial message. They must specifically opt-in, if not from CAN-SPAM rules than from most email service provider's terms of service. The second challenge is the time and effort, therefore hard cost and expense, of creating meaningful, timely, and relevant content for the potential recipients of the trickle campaign. The analysis of a sample email campaign showed that creation of one email blast for the entire file can be cost prohibitive, now do the same calculations on an even smaller number of prospects.

When considering the average size of business email lists and the pace at which new opted-in emails are added, the appeal of trickle email marketing decreases dramatically. The cost required to develop a campaign for a few people every month precludes most businesses from pursuing this strategy, no matter the appeal. At low volumes calling is more effective. For those firms that have the ability to generate the necessary flow of new leads, trickle marketing can be a powerful tool in the arsenal. For most of businesses, this promise is just software vendor hype.

Maximizing Email ROI

There are steps that a marketer can take to maximize the return generated by email. Email campaigns must be considered a part of the overall marketing strategy and need to be coordinated across all channels. Consider the following to develop an effective email program:

▸ Offer customers the opportunity to join the email list at every marketing and sales touch point

▸ Create campaigns that are designed to collect email addresses – many people will trade their personal information for a pittance

▸ Utilize easy to complete opt-in forms on landing pages and shopping carts

▸ Utilize Personalized URLs (PURLs) with email to drive respondents to a content specific landing page to help increase conversion

▸ Send email infrequently with relevant and timely content targeted at the individual recipient

THE WORST EMAIL CAMPAIGN EVER

It is often impossible to get IT and IS to support marketing efforts and it is very typical for customer information to be housed in a tangled mess of legacy systems and data silos. Even in large, technically savvy organizations, front line staff responsible for particular marketing efforts or product lines do not have access corporate IT support. The fact of the matter is that customers do not care about data challenges. Internecine struggles over turf and a firm's innate inability to know about its own business and customer base is no excuse to fail to execute. The stakeholders that the management team serves, and the clients they sell to, will not believe that getting the marketing basics of tackling and blocking are too hard.

Mercedes Benz, a firm with vast marketing resources, should win the award for producing the worst email campaign ever. It was not just that the design was poorly done and the artwork came through horribly pixilated. It was not that most of the content was irrelevant to the model of car my family has in the garage and it was not even that disclaimers outweighed content by more two to one.

What makes this tragic marketing effort the worst email ever sent is that there was no call to action. Despite the horrid construction of the email, the offer was still compelling. But alas, there were no links, no phone numbers, and no way to make a purchase. There was not even a note to contact your local dealer.

But wait, there's more. On the company's website (www.mbusa. com) there is no search bar and the product line being offered in the email did not appear in the site map or anywhere else on the web that could be found after extensive effort to do so. The local dealer, when called about the offer, had no idea what it was! How many customers will pay attention to the next offer after an experience like that?

Lessons Learned

The first step in any marketing plan is to have good data before you do anything else. This is especially true if you have detailed records like a car company or bank. Your customers don't care about data silos, turf wars, and legal tangles like the Health Insurance Portability and Accountability Act of 1996 (HIPPA). They pay you and they expect you to know who they are. Period.

There is no excuse to not know your customer. Big firms are the worst at this. It is critical for marketers not to send content to customers that is not relevant – it just confirms the notion that firm does not care. Never offer your customers accessories for a car they don't own or an invitation to apply for a credit card that they already have. The best course of action is to kill the campaign and invest elsewhere if the data is not available.

Assure that your offer always has a clear call to action. Make sure that the ways to purchase the product or service offered are very clear. There is nothing more frustrating than not being able to find out how to take the next step. Do not make the customer think. Make the way to buy or take action obvious. Always include a customer service number or email for help and seriously reconsider the marketing effort if you cannot support your offer. Why risk a short term bump in revenue or traffic at the risk of alienating customers?

Companies routinely squander good will by providing bad customer experiences. Every customer touch is equally important and should be treated as such. Be certain your fulfillment channel knows that you are making an offer and what the offer is, before you hit the send button. There is no excuse not to coordinate efforts no matter how big the firm. Send less if necessary, but send right.

These sound like common sense things to do, but large consumer firms as diverse as Mercedes Benz, Bank of America, AT&T, Xerox and Sprint routinely send out marketing communications that have no relevance to the recipient or even worse, contain offers which the recipient does not even qualify for. Your customers will remember the insults when it comes time to renew or expand the relationship.

Cross Media Channels Part II 5

Cross Media Channels Part II

SHORT MESSAGE SERVICE (SMS TEXT)

Short Message Service (SMS Text) is a mobile phone driven application that sends text messages to recipients who have specifically opt to receive them. The most common ways to gather mobile phone numbers is to sponsor a contest, create a loyalty program, or offer exclusive content or alerts. The technology is based on a "short code" that is licensed in the United States from the Federal Government through the Common Short Code Administration (CSCA).

A short code is either five or six digits that mobile companies know is assigned to a particular marketer much like a phone number. An example SMS campaign might be "Text CASH to 55512 for a chance to win $5000." Once cell numbers are collected, consumers can be invited to opt-in for communications and their phone number can be appended for contact and demographic information.

The rules for gathering and sending mobile marketing messages are not as highly regulated as email, but they are just as difficult to comply with. Cellular companies act as de facto regulators with rules found in their terms of service. There is not an equivalent federal law for SMS Text as there is for email. General provisions of the United States Code prevent the sending of unsolicited text messages. There is ongoing controversy over whether the Federal Communications Commission should treat short codes as a regulated common carrier telecom service or as a largely unregulated information service. Each wireless network has varying rules and standards that aggregators who offer text services must wade through. The network owners act as gatekeepers on content they allow on their systems and have denied access to certain organizations for political and competitive issues.

The Common Short Code Administration (CSCA), Mobile Marketing Association (MMA) and industry association CITA all influence the use of short codes. These organizations provide "best practices" and recommended content uses on their websites. Links to their websites are provided in Appendix C.

Shared vs. Unique Short Codes

Many firms wish to dip their toe in the water when it comes to SMS text in order to minimize cost. A dedicated short code will have an upfront cost as high as $30,000 and monthly minimums in the range of $3,000 to $5,000. There are various firms that offer shared short codes in which a service provider owns the Federal license for the code and then allows multiple advertisers to use it for their campaigns. A marketer can rent a keyword for that code, "win" for example, and all responses containing that keyword will be flagged to that organization's campaign.

The Benefits of Mobile Marketing with SMS Text

✔ **Speed and Ease of Execution**

Mobile Campaigns are simple to set up, with messages being delivered almost immediately.

✔ **Affordability**

When using a shared short code there is no need to pay for postage or air time, just a nominal per text message fee. Many vendors have systems that are volume driven and feature "pay as you go" options to minimize up front costs, and keep deployment charges nominal.

✔ **Span and Reach**

Reach out to people all over the world. Delivery rates are extraordinarily high and recipients do not require a smart phone to receive content.

✔ **Response Rate**

Announcements at events can yield 40 to 60% and subsequent touches can yield 3 to 5 times the responses generated by other efforts.

✔ **Personalization**

Create campaigns that are driven by variable content and provide a personal experience to the specific user. Take marketing campaigns to the next level by adding SMS Text messaging to increase the opt-in response rate.

> For serious use of this channel, a dedicated short code is strongly recommended which makes the cost rise significantly. Assume approximately $35,000 will be required to own and operate a code for one year.

The mobile providers and aggregators who deal with the cellular companies do not like shared short codes because content and SPAM control become exponentially more difficult. From the marketer's perspective, there is a risk involved with the low cost shared option. A violation by one user of the shared code could result in the code being shut off. For any multi-channel campaign, or even a single channel campaign with any longevity, the chance that the code may also be used by a bar or strip club and that unscrupulous users may cause the code to be terminated are important considerations.

SMS Text is currently one of the least used of the cross media channels and perhaps the easiest in which to build an opt-in marketing list. The "text to win" campaign is the most common but updates on virtually any aspect of a product or service can be offered. SMS Text messages reach recipients wherever they are and there is no need to have access to a TV, radio, computer, or mailbox. This strategy is particularly useful for outdoor events, stadiums, tracks, raceways and other popular venues. Airports, bus stops, and any other waiting areas provide people the opportunity to take immediate action. Virtually all cellular phones, even older and the most basic models, are SMS Text capable.

The most powerful use of SMS text is at widely attended events where immediate opt-ins can be accomplished. The offer can be made via handouts, public address announcements, and presentation on the large video displays at field houses and stadiums. When combined with a desirable offer that is not readily available for purchase, this channel can generate massive numbers of leads in an electronic format, much more quickly than a booth or other experiential format. The key to success is the relevancy and rarity of the offer. It does not need to be an expensive prize – what fan wouldn't opt-in for the chance to win the signed jersey of the game's MVP or the game ball?

Data collected from the SMS campaign can be easily appended with name and address information from a variety of consumer databases giving the marketer an interested base of prospects for direct marketing. The tie-in from the recent event will definitely help the piece survive the mail moment. SMS Text is an easy way to leverage other forms of marketing to gain an immediate response.

MOBILE MARKETING & QR CODES

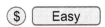

There are numerous ways that marketers can use mobile technology to deliver marketing messages and start two-way conversations. Email and SMS Text can be used on mobile devices, and each are handled in their own sections of this chapter. The primary advantage of mobile marketing is that the recipient of the marketing message usually has the response device on hand, even while shopping, travelling, at work or at an event for business or pleasure.

Internet enabled camera phones can take a picture of this graphic and have information uploaded to their device without the need to type a web address.

QR Codes

There are several methods that can be used to drive prospects to mobile content. "Quick Response" or QR Codes are two dimensional, machine readable graphics that encode data. The data encoded in a QR Code may include letters, text, numbers, URLs and files. QR Codes are particularly popular in Japan and are growing in popularity elsewhere. QR Codes can be displayed anywhere that a graphic can appear, from a sign at a bus stop to a paid online ad. Respondents can access information by taking

87

a picture of the code with a reader, often included or available as a downloaded application on a camera equipped cell phone. Every reader acts in a slightly different way so it is important to test the code on a variety of devices and applications.

QR Codes can be incorporated into any web mix and can be generated for free at numerous sites online. They are used to add an additional response mechanism to other channels in order to get information quickly onto the target's mobile device. When using this response mechanism, be sure to track respondents that utilize the codes and segment which channel they prefer. Avoid data silos while collecting data and coordinate all channels by using the code to access a mobile enhanced landing page in order to continue the opt-in and two-way conversation process.

The most useful way to implement a QR Code as part of a campaign is to use a dedicated landing page to act as a collection mechanism. For variable marketing applications such as email or variable data print, individual codes can be generated for each recipient. This code can contain a Personalized URL (PURL) or other specific content, such as a prize or discount code.

Landing Page Design For Mobile

The sales and marketing leader needs to keep a few design ideas in mind when planning for mobile content. The first choice to make is whether to change the style sheet for the web site in question or to produce a whole separate set of content. One example is http://www.vdpweb.com versus http://m.vdpweb.com for mobile content. The site can also automatically detect the type of browser being used and serve mobile content, but be sure to have an easy way to access the main site for those who have large viewing areas on their mobile devices. Tablet PC and iPad users will want the option of accessing the main site even though they are using a mobile browser.

Since the QR Code is most likely to be accessed by mobile device, the content needs to take this into account. Some mobile browsers are able to expand and pan, but many cannot. A few specific suggestions include:

▸ Keep the design simple and bold for easy viewing and navigation

▸ Avoid using wide images and adding content to the page which requires a large amounts of bandwidth

▸ Use basic design elements with minimal styling to create menus and buttons instead of images

▸ Remember that different mobile browsers or QR Code readers will override some site code (such as scaling), so keep it simple

▸ Some QR Code readers, such as Mobile Tag on the iPhone, add a query string onto the URL which can cause issues with some sites

MOBILE VIDEO

Until recently, mobile video was a method of marketing that has been the purview of specialty firms, usually created on behalf of large entertainment and sports clients. Hollywood movie studios, television networks and major entertainment franchises are about the only ones who have committed the resources to create the specialized content. The format and resolution of the files limit its use in other channels as the content has very specific requirements. Most budget conscious marketers rely on web video as discussed in the next section.

Despite the popularity of the iPhone and iPad, they are by no means the only media capable devices. There are numerous platforms with varying operating systems, screen resolutions, sizes, and content parameters that make the development of mobile content very expensive. Additionally, the more limited reach of this channel for general business to business and consumer sales makes it cost far more than other parts of the media mix.

WEB VIDEO

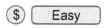

Many firms have turned to video as a principle means of presenting the elevator pitch for products and services. Frequently asked questions (FAQs), or technical demonstrations and feature presentations are popular topics for video in efforts to decrease the number of customer service hours necessary to support clients.

Video Spokesperson

One of the easiest and most cost effective ways to produce content is to employ a video spokesperson where a script is provided to a third party provider. These services use an actor to present the video content and return a snippet of code that can be embedded on virtually any web page. This technique is no more difficult to execute than producing a fifteen or thirty second radio spot. Various online services provide this product at an out the door cost of less than $500.

Video Blogs

Successful video content does not necessarily require a big budget and slick production values. Desktop cameras with short, unscripted vignettes are authentic and engaging, especially when they come from senior company leaders. Technical perfection is not required in the shorts. The videos can be hosted on free web sites such as YouTube which provides easy to use embed code that includes a player. Some experts believe that video content will become increasingly important in naturalized search results in the coming years.

Here are a few suggestions for getting the best results from video presentations.

1. Do not automatically play the audio/visual portion of web content. A window or graphic can be conspicuously placed that advises the visitor that the video is present, but does not force them to view the content. It is impossible to judge a visitor's preference so it is likely better to err on the side of caution. Web visitor's who shut off a video because they are frustrated by the intrusion are less likely to continue viewing the site or watching the video content later. Additionally, after the second visit to the site, the auto-playing movie can be downright annoying. In the same vein, do not repeat the movie with auto-play on multiple pages.

2. Like any other advertising channel, make sure the video content is relevant and timely to the audience. If in doubt as to what demographic will be visiting the site, concentrate the video on landing pages that are geared to particular demographics.

3. Keep the content on the videos fresh.

4. Do not rely on video content at the expense of quality copy. The visitor may or may not be receptive to audio-visual content and it is difficult to skim a video.

UNIQUE PHONE NUMBERS

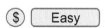 $ Easy

The use of unique phone numbers for campaigns has been in use for years. This technique provides valuable insight as to the source of leads and the channel that reached them. Despite its proven value and ease of execution, very few campaigns employ this technology.

Voice over Internet Provider (VOIP) allows for the easy execution of unique phone numbers used for tracking by campaign without the need to add traditional phone lines. The numbers can be rented at low cost with no long term commitments from a variety of providers. The unique number routes the call (passes the call through) to the appropriate place and records key data such as call time, duration, etc. These numbers can be used to measure channel efficacy in the same way as a unique URL. Data can be appended from consumer databases to add demographic information.

SEARCH ENGINE OPTIMIZATION

Fresh content, relevance, and traffic are the keys to the success of any website in search. One easy way to determine how the firm's offerings are positioned in the marketplace is to examine the search terms that are driving traffic to the web site. Are the phrases being used driven towards the conceptual or practical? Are visitors searching for awareness or detail? What stage of product life cycle is your vertical in? What part of buying cycle is your customer in? The answers to these questions will determine the content required.

Prior to the Internet

In traditional marketing practice, advertising captured leads after prospects were convinced to take some action which led to a purchase or sales call. The methods of tracking response were either difficult to execute or required massive infrastructure investment in point of sale or corporate CRM computer systems. Access to the data once it was finally collected was difficult and often siloed by vertical. Access remains impossible in many organizations.

Early Internet: Web 1.0

Search and opt-ins were the only way to capture traffic. A prospect had to fill out a form or make a phone call from information that was presented on a corporate website. Internet connections were slow, and internet service providers such as America Online had significant influence over content and how it was presented. Search engines such as Google were not yet the key locators of content.

Current Internet: Web 2.0

Search and social media now equally drive traffic. It is critical that companies maintain social media content such as a blog, LinkedIn, and Facebook accounts much in the same way that firms used to need a website to prove the were legitimate and reputable players. The use of social media is a business requirement to be competitive in any market space and it is not optional if the firm wants to be taken seriously. From the largest corporations conducting spin on their media coverage to the corner bakery "twittering" to followers that fresh cookies are coming out of the oven, the value of creating two-way conversations with clients can not be overlooked.

The key factors that determine a web site's performance in a nationalized search for particular keywords are generally well accepted. The vast majority of rankings are determined by four things.

▸ Age of the site and amount of content

▸ Traffic and links to relevant content

▸ Relevance of content to the search terms

▸ Up-to-date content

There are other factors to consider for search engine optimization and these tend to change frequently. The presence of video and certain other types of social media content may weigh more heavily in the months and years to come.

Other Factors

If your number one keyword is in your web address, you have a leg up in the naturalized search. Search engines use "web crawlers" or "bots", short for code robots, to explore internet content and assign values. Although the exact algorithms of the process are hidden, here are a few simple things that can be done to a company web site in order to begin the ongoing process of moving the site higher in the search engines/rankings.

Page Titles

Many experts believe that this is the most important part of search engine optimization. It is critical to write accurate, keyword rich page titles. The copy that appears in the page title must also appear in the content. For example, a weak title would be Acme Manufacturing Home Page. A stronger home page title would include important key words a prospect will search for. Acme Conveyor Belts, Parts and Service is much stronger.

Meta Descriptions

This is how a site is described in search engines. If the site does not have a description, the search engines will just pull the first bit of content off the page in order to determine what the content of the page contains. Again, make the meta descriptors keyword-rich and keep the terms less than 160 characters long.

Descriptive URLS

Don't use a generic URL that features code or cryptic messages like Acme.com/fgfgfh.php/code.aspx. Instead, name the URL with a searchable term like Acme.com/conveyorbeltparts.aspx.

Meta Tags

These tags are the keywords that appear in web page coding to inform search engines of the site's keywords. These tags may not be as important as they once were, but it is still easy to include this content on the page. Most experts believe these tags will continue to have some importance for search engines.

Replace Flash and Images with Text

If the site relies on links or headings which are displayed as images, search engines can not read the content. Replace as many as possible with text to improve readability. Flash-based websites offer very little in the way for search engine bots to crawl and rank low due to small amounts of text.

Create an XML Sitemap for the Website

This informs search engines about URLs on a website that are available for crawling. To create a free sitemap for your website visit: www.xml-sitemaps.com.

The balance and weight given to different factors are constantly changing in the algorithms of the search engines. Two trends are currently useful for helping to produce high ranking "page one" results.

Blog Content

Blogging software firms are currently weighed very heavily by search engines. This is a function of their high volume and freshness of content as numerous authors constantly post to their sites. The content may not remain highly ranked for long, but steady generation of content can keep your brand on the first page of the various search engines. This content can feature links to your website to boost a firm's web presence.

Video for Naturalized Search

The weight given to sites that contain video content and the video content in and of itself seems to be gaining in importance in the major search engine algorithms. Video links will sometimes appear as a separate entry above web content links to the same subject matter. This makes the inclusion of video more important than in years past. As mentioned previously, the movies produced do not need to be expensive, high end productions to have the desired effect.

Naturalized Search Services

There are many firms and services that offer guaranteed placement on the first page Google for a monthly subscription fee. Be very wary of these. They usually operate by creating a few keyword search phrases that are tangentially related to your desired terms and focus on getting these to the top of the rankings. These phrases may be maneuvered into a good ranking, but be sure they are actually the searches being used by prospects who are doing the searching. The weakness of these services is that the usually do not focus on the key elements of naturalized search – fresh, relevant content and traffic. The creation of new content and its distribution are critical. Some of these service charge outrageous amounts for very little work.

PAID SEARCH

There have been thousands of books, blogs, and "how to's" written about paid search advertising. There is no need to repeat the minutia of that content here. From the perspective of the marketing and sales leader, budget and effectiveness are the two major issues. In addition to a large budget in order to compete for popular words, there are several things that can be done to maximize paid search return. Paid search must be leveraged with data collection mechanisms to maximize its value. Drive respondents to a landing page and start two-way conversations.

The True Cost of Pay-per-Click

It is critical for marketers to determine the click through and conversion rates for their paid search campaigns. The two examples shown below are not uncommon results for many firms. The cost per click charge on many keywords has reached ludicrous heights. The costs for the two examples that follow are not unreasonable.

Business to Business Example:

Search Term	Cost Per Click	% Opt-In	Cost per Lead
Marketing	$24.00	1.0%	$2,4000

Business to Consumer Example:

Search Term	Cost Per Click	% Purchase	Cost per Sale
Briefcase	$14.00	1.0%	$140.00

In the business to business example the cost per lead is astronomical. Popular search terms frequently run more than $20

99

per click and $50 or more is becoming common with some as high as $100. For sales with large revenue and high margins it may be possible to absorb the expense. Other firms see the exorbitant price tag as a cost of doing business to capture market share. For most businesses, pay per click campaigns can be very risky ventures.

If the average cost of a briefcase sold is $200, then a $140 cost per sale means the bag is being sold at a large loss. This is a typical result for many internet advertisers who hope that by capturing a customer they can develop marketing leads that will result in repeat purchases without the high cost of acquisition. If the average ticket of a sale is small, then paid search can quickly become cost prohibitive.

ONLINE MEETINGS, WEBINARS & SEMINARS

$ [Easy] to $ $ [Moderate]

Marketing messages on any channel can feature an online event as the call to action. Several software as a service providers allow webinars to be economically held. Access to the software can be acquired for monthly a subscription that costs between $50 and $150 dollars depending on the number of participants required.

Use social media, press releases, and other viral channels to advertise your event at a small cost. Even if attendance is low, the long term effect of the web content created for hosting the event can provide dividends years after the date has passed. The content for these sessions can include:

▸ Industry trends and predictions

▸ Best practices

▸ Expert guest speakers

▸ Case studies

▸ How to demonstrations

▸ Sales presentations

These events are often most successful as a "soft sell" that positions the firm as a reliable source of information and expertise. Avoid the almost overwhelming temptation to make a hard sales pitch. If an attendee is interested in the product or service, they will find it.

DATA COLLECTION – TRADE SHOWS & EVENTS

 ⓢ ⓢ [Moderate]

Trade shows and special events provide the perfect venues to utilize cross media marketing applications. The data collection point can be an unmanned kiosk rented specifically for the purpose or laptops and workstations connected to a WiFi or cellular network.

Chicago Event – On Site Collection Page

A Chicago event marketing agency hosted a fabulous event for the trade at 1028 Hooker in Chicago in 2009. The goal was more than to have a great function. The party hostesses used a tablet PC (an iPad is equally good) and a landing page to gather emails, cell phone numbers and opt-ins for promotions and messaging from the guests. The dark pad and trendy page were well received, looked very cool, and drew a crowd each time the hostess stopped to get a survey completed. A thank you message automatically fired to the respondent via text and email. Many were received on mobile devices while they were still at the event. The hosts could process about twenty opt-ins per hour.

The contact, opt-in, and survey information was delivered directly into the agency's data base of prospects. The information could be used to send follow up direct marketing via SMS Text, email, and direct mail to the opt-ins gathered by the hostesses. Although the page design was very basic, this process is a powerful and simple data collection and brand building mechanism for any special event such as a trade show, shopping mall promotion, charity activity and more. Data collection rates, including the time spent circulating around the space and chatting with guests was one survey every three minutes. This is a very efficient means of collecting vital demographic and survey information while building a relationship the prospect will remember. Best of all, the cost of developing the entire system was less than the cost of a few extra guests at the bar.

MarketVision stand-alone kiosk (photo courtesy of CIK Enterprises)

Various firms offer the rental of stand-alone kiosks for the collection of opt-ins that do not require the presence of staff. Many people do not desire to interact directly with sales people and prefer to engage electronically, even at a live event. The kiosk can be used to register for the event, collect opt-ins and sweepstakes entries, and conduct surveys. Many trade shows offer badge scanners and other collection mechanisms as part of the exhibitor package or as an option. A kiosk may still be of value even if these other mechanisms are implemented. Responders can be kept confidential from third party event organizers and add custom functionality, such as printing a ticket or prize form. Additionally, data can be exported directly into the firm's cross media platform thereby avoiding a data silo.

POINT OF SALE

The main challenge in conducting cross media marketing and opt-ins at the point of sale location is the cost of implementation of tools that provide adequate speed and data flow. In this case, small firms with a small number of locations are at a distinct advantage over larger competitors. It may be impossible for The Home Depot to quickly collect survey and opt-in data at the register with legacy point of sale systems, but the corner hardware store, which is often using a standalone PC or local server for point of sale, can easily add a data collection landing page with only web access required to execute.

The challenge for most small firms will be consistency in getting the staff to collect the surveys from shoppers. Many organizations have slips of paper or a book that is used for gathering email and postal address which are used to send newsletters and special offers. A landing page allows for the immediate entry of contacts into the database and avoids another data silo. Firms hampered by legacy point of sale systems can use a kiosk as described in the previous section to accomplish the same thing. A single unit can be placed near the exit or after the checkout line in big box retailers, grocery store chains, and similar brick and mortar outlets.

CALL CENTERS

 Moderate

Firms that rely on call centers for ordering, customer service or other uses can leverage the incoming phone number to help create an actionable database of customers to contact via direct marketing. For years, data appends have been used by large firms to generate data on callers, but the internet makes it possible for any size firm to leverage external data sources without extensive investment in specialized computer systems or point of sale hardware. Combine the call center with a unique phone number and real time personalization in order to maximize its lead generation potential.

The process for utilizing a call center for data collection and marketing purposes can be divided into three steps. The first step is the data collection process by real time personalization.

Step two uses this profile to generate a persona based on the results. Specific offers can be made while the prospect is still on the phone. Finally, the personal and demographic information acquired can be used as the basis for a direct marketing communication. This final touch, which can be part of an automated process, can return very high results.

CUSTOMER RELATIONSHIP MANAGEMENT (CRM)

Developing a customer relationship management system was once the most daunting challenge of many sales and marketing organizations. The main goal must be to feed data from all sources into centralized location. One the keys to success of this aspect of the cross media strategy is that there must be minimal ongoing organization effort required for execution. The more effort that is required on behalf of sales forces or other individuals in the organization on a regular basis the more likely the project is to fail. Asking already overworked employees to add another task that takes "just five minutes per day" will rarely succeed. The key for marketers is to set up processes that funnel data into the CRM from activities that are already being executed.

Logging phone calls, sales notes, and customer comments can be expected and controlled from call center employees sitting in front of terminals all day, but many communications fall outside easy to enter systems. Cross media applications can feed into the sales funnel in an automated way. By driving respondents to the web from multiple channels, consistent data can be collected in a centralized location and this database can interact directly with the CRM.

CRM systems used to be cost prohibitive to implement and customize. Many firms now offer reasonably priced and powerful software as a service customer relationship management systems such as Salesforce.com and dozens of others. These web based solutions can be accessed from any internet connection and allow small firms powerful tools to customize processes. The most important factor in choosing a CRM provider is the avail-ability of access to the database and its ability to easily accept data from the cross media marketing efforts. This will help avoid sales and marketing data being disjointed. Most systems have an Application Programming Interface (API) that allows for data to be automatically communicated to eliminate data silos.

Social Media **6**

Social Media

Hype aside, social media is an important marketing tool that can play an important role in a lead generation strategy. Like email, the creation and deployment of social media campaigns is not free. There is either going to be vast amounts of time or money thrown at the project. The most effective social media efforts have content provided by the highest echelons of the firm. A CEO's blog is likely to be better received than one created and written by sales staff or a marketing firm. Can sincerity be faked? Maybe. But readers are savvy and selective and the backlash could be huge.

The evidence of the power of social media is all around. Take ten minutes to sit in the typical urban coffee shop and you will see patrons with laptops and smart phones at work or play. It is likely that some will have headphones on and that most have not paid for the vast majority of the content they are utilizing. Every year, fewer and fewer people are reading magazines or newspapers. Even the television is being ignored if there is one at all. Can there be any doubt that social media applications are needed to reach people?

The most important factor in any cross media marketing strategy is content. The creation of timely and relevant material that influencers and potential customers want to read and share will be the key to success regardless of the channels or applications currently in vogue. The problem is that online content is not free to produce or distribute, but consumers are reluctant to pay for it and many are not willing to tolerate invasive advertising. Disseminating information throughout the sales cycle is critical and how each channel contributes to the sale needs to be reviewed.

The outlets that are popular in Web 2.0 are not the same as those from Web 1.0. The content owners and influencers of the past were names like AOL, Yahoo, and PRWeb. Remember keywords for AOL? Today, Facebook has displaced MySpace for both personal and professional usage, Twitter and LinkedIn are among those that dominate business social media, and press releases are a quaint side note that are primarily covered on other channels. The trend will always be for newcomers to seek out the next big thing so that they can compete with the entrenched leaders. This keeps the landscape fluid and gives new firms a chance to overtake established players in the market. This also means that there will be a constant struggle to stay on top.

Popularity is Fine, Results are Better

A popular internet campaign in 2008 was an amazingly clever gag viral marketing piece about a coffee making, harmonica based smart phone that leads to a very serious website for Discover Nova Scotia. The goal was for firms considering a move to consider relocation to consider this Maritime Province. After spending a significant amount of time at the site (www.pomegranatephone.com) and being very entertained, I asked myself a few questions. Did spending a virtual fortune on the production of this interactive site really translate into leads for the Province of Nova Scotia? Did all this effort get the right

111

people to the final content? The same budget spent on direct marketing to target businesses would likely yield more inquiries. How many decision making executives could have been touched directly with a variable data communication targeted to their sector, a personalized landing page, and robust tracking by prospect's name and position? Popularity is fine but measurable results are better.

It is safe to assume that customer bandwidth will not increase over time as there are only so many hours in the day. There is a plateau of efficiency that has been reached by the end users of content. As the amount of available information continues to increase, the accessibility of any one marketing or sales organization's content will continue to decline. There is a clear need to develop leadership in select content areas and channels. The key to success will be developing leadership in a few critical content areas and channels. It will be impossible to be a leader in every category so the channel selection process is the main factor in the cross media process.

A major goal of social media must be to get bloggers, analysts, and other market influencers to have a conversation and have that conversation be found by your customer. In many cases the buyer and decision-maker is not the end user of a product or service. It is critical to target the end-user in order to influence decision maker. Firms can help set the buying criteria in the market that matches your product features by controlling, or at least influencing, the online dialogue. Executives, sales, marketing, and support staff must all be actively involved to keep clients happy and to find competitor clients who are unhappy.

Social media is more than brand building. Web 2.0 applications are necessary to position the firm as a thought leader and trusted content source in the vertical. Social media can make significant contributions in the business to business sales process by establishing and maintaining the company reputation and providing leads for the sales pipeline. Social media content is always "out there" for the asking and it can be repurposed to any channel.

STARTING OFF IN SOCIAL MEDIA

Ideally, a full-time corporate communications professional with exceptional writing skills, a solid background in the appropriate product vertical, and experience in social media would be tasked with maintaining the firm's cross channel marketing efforts. The number of such positions actually staffed must be miniscule in compared to the need. The reality is that marketing departments, whose staff counts have been decimated by the recent economic downturn, must rely on fewer internal resources to expand the company presence in more channels. Here are the first three steps to take to engage a firm in social media without dedicating more resources to the task.

1. Start at the Top

To many business experts, the principal job of the Chief Executive Officer, President, and Vice President of Marketing in any firm is to be the CIC – Cheerleader in Chief. Content that is written by company leaders is the most valuable marketing tool a firm has in social media. The insights of the top brass go a long way in the reader's eye. The content is taken as being more

113

meaningful. Yes, the boss is busy and he will not want to take time to pontificate on the business rather than running it. That being said, executive content is a key element in both customer and employee loyalty and confidence. By keeping all stakeholders in the loop and providing a two-way conversation with these constituents, business leaders can gain valuable insight into both the market and their operations in addition to building brand and driving sales.

This strategy is not without a downside. Flippant remarks, inaccurate information, and even corporate strategy could slip into the mix and cause damage to the brand. In most cases, the rewards far outweigh the risks. While executives need to avoid arguing with readers or responding directly to spurious attacks, they can address the issues relevant to all stakeholders in a less formal, more intimate way. A portion of the content must come (or appear to come) from outside of the marketing and sales functions.

2. Leverage

Sales and Marketing Executives need to leverage existing campaigns, copy, and art by adapting them to different media. This sounds obvious enough, but in many cases each campaign or initiative leads to a new set of creative. The larger the organization the more likely this is to occur. Even when there is a brand manual available, the design process is usually started over from scratch. By reusing content the cost of entering a new channel is decreased significantly.

The most important step in leveraging data is to assure that all content is stored in a centralized location. This includes not only digital or hard copies of what went out, but also the complete, original design files for the content. A PDF proof from the printer does not constitute having access to past campaigns. This step is especially critical if an agency or other third party was involved in the design process. Even if these other parties follow the brand manual, the content they create will still take hours to reproduce assuming that the firm has the ability in-house.

3. Multi Use Design

When it is necessary to create new content for the campaign, keep the design limitations of other channels in mind. There are design elements that are fine in print that are impossible to reproduce on the web.

Social Media User Information

The following is a summary of interesting survey data from the Social Media Marketing Industry Report by Michael A. Stelzner.

The top three questions marketers want answered are: What are the best tactics to use? How is the effectiveness of social media measured? Where is the best place to start?

Marketers are mostly new to social media but 88% of marketers surveyed are using social media to market their businesses. 72% of respondents have only been using social media marketing channels for a few months or less.

64% of marketers are using social media for 5 hours or more each week and 39% are using social media for 10 or more hours weekly.

81% of marketers report that the top benefit of social media marketing is generating exposure for the business. Other responses include increasing traffic and building new business partnerships.

 Twitter, blogs, LinkedIn and Facebook were the top four social media tools used by marketers, in that order. The social media tools marketers most wanted to learn about were bookmarking sites and Twitter.

The responses given highlight the value that marketing and sales executives place on the implementation of social media. Even those business leaders that have no interest in these channels will find that stakeholders from the board room to the end user will demand their utilization.

Buyers today are fundamentally different than they were only ten years ago. The way both business buyers and consumers learn about products and services has changed dramatically. Information on organizations and the competition is readily available and side by side comparisons are easy to do. Sales is no longer required to act as the main conduit of information to educate clients. The web now does that anonymously. Therefore, the only way to understand the virtual sales process is to track and measure buyer activity online to gauge their level of interest.

The Top Cross Media Marketing Mistakes

✔ Not starting immediately

✔ Not coordinating across channels and brands

✔ Not providing a centralized data collection mechanism

✔ Creating data silos of response metrics and opt-ins

✔ Failing to start a two-way conversation

✔ Not asking questions and seeking customer input

✔ Not letting the customer choose the communications channel and frequency

Social media marketing can also help bring sales and marketing into alignment. Tracking online activity allows the firm to enter the sales cycle at the right time by tracking activity. Clean and consistent data collection is the key to social media marketing. For any organization with any type of sales cycle the goal is to determine where the prospect or buyer came from and why they got to the page that they did. Firms need to know what the point of referral was.

SOCIAL MEDIA CHANNELS

There are hundreds of social media channels available. Even with unlimited resources it would be impossible to dominate them all. The choices range from review sites and directories to blogs and virtual communities. The following channels and strategies are recommended for the average firm or a department in a larger organization without access to enterprise resources. The selections are designed to be implemented without leaders having to commit significant resources to the project.

Choosing a Social Media & Networking Channel

There are an almost infinite number of cross media channels available from general interest to hyper-targeted segments of particular verticals. Several of the channels below were not intended as marketing tools but have become lifestyle influencers that marketers have tapped into. The general idea is to create a wide net of sites and content on various engines so that the firm, product, or service can be more easily found in naturalized search. The ultimate goal is to be the central hub of the conversation about your vertical. The more locations and links a firm has, the easier it will be for decision makers to find.

BLOGGING

Corporate communications need a centralized repository that can be linked to and easily found. The initial inclination may be to host the blog on the company's main site. The advantage to that method is to provide fresh content as frequently as posts are made. The challenge for many firms is that the web site is not easy to change internally with any frequency and it may be difficult to add content management functionality to the site. Smaller firms with low traffic may do far better in naturalized search by leveraging the rankings of blog software providers.

Where to Locate the Blog

A blog can be hosted almost anywhere and various providers offer software as a service solutions to provide the content management at a very reasonable price. The advantage of using a paid service such as TypePad or WordPress is that search engines, specifically Google, index the material almost immediately. This pays huge dividends for naturalized search results. The content of the blog can be fed by Really Simple Syndication (RSS Feed) into the corporate site. An example can be found at www.vdpweb.com/blog.

High placement may be short lived for any particular article, but the results can be immediate and fresh content can always be added to keep the product or service coming up in the first page of carefully selected keywords.

119

LINKEDIN

If a business leader has only one presence on the web this site should be it. LinkedIn is a business-focused social network that joins individuals to others by means of professional introductions and interest groups. As of December 2010, there are more than 85,000,000 members. According to the company, a new member joins LinkedIn every second, and about half of the members are located outside of the United States. This is the most popular site of its type. Others include ZoomInfo, Chamber.com, and the European XING.

In both LinkedIn home pages and groups, conversations can be started that seek input from other users. Groups are particularly valuable for beginning two-way conversations. Participants are easily identified and can become prospects. Firms can create user moderated groups around topics or even products and services. It is becoming increasingly common for a firm or individual to be researched on LinkedIn as part of the due diligence process. A complete profile that has a substantial network and recommendations goes a long way toward establishing gravitas and credibility in many verticals, especially those that require a particular expertise. A professional social media presence is as important to many sales processes as a corporate and product website.

FACEBOOK

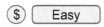

Originally intended as a way for college students to connect and interact, Facebook has become almost ubiquitous among teens and a vast number of adults. 85% of college students are believed to have profiles on the site and the average age of users continue to increase. As of March 2010, Facebook had more than 111,200,000 users.

At the time this book was published, Mashable reports that more than 50 million accounts are held by active users and 35 million of these update their pages each day. More than 23 million users are over the age of 35. More than 6.5 million are over the age of 55. This is obviously not a medium only for teens and twenty-somethings and it cannot be ignored by business leaders.

Screenshot of company Facebook page

Facebook Statistics

Users	111,200,000
US	23,500,000
Indonesia	19,500,000
Turkey	18,700,000
France	16,000,000
Active Users	50,000,000
Daily Users	35,000,000
Average Minutes per Day	35
Average Comments per Month	25
Groups Joined	13
Pages Visited per Month	4

Facebook for Companies

Facebook offers "Fan Pages" where companies and products can be featured. Marketers can use other channels to attract a network of fans who can comment and build buzz around a product or service. This process is probably most effective for cultural events such as movies, books, television shows and popular consumer products, although other businesses are getting attention on the site. The same process for both personal and business content can be used on other social media sites.

MYSPACE

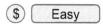

Another popular social media site is MySpace, once the leader in social networking. Its user network has declined in North America but continues to be wildly popular in various parts of the world. The application runs in much the same way as Facebook with accounts and profiles.

TWITTER

This social media site is a wonder. The premise is to send SMS type text messages called "tweets" to a network of followers and to receive short messages from people whose activities you follow. The idea seemed ludicrous to many at first. For marketing and sales, the use of the site transformed from sending personal notes and comments to a powerful business tool. By sending links to interesting content to a network of followers, businesses can build a loyal group of fans that can then be served announcements about the vertical, product or service.

In many ways, Twitter emulates a blog by providing a title and links to content that users can follow without the effort of extensive content development. The individuals and groups that follow your activity become warm leads.

Twitter for Lead Generation

By monitoring who follows your "tweets" and contacting these prospects directly from the information located in their profile, Twitter can be a powerful lead generation tool. The utility offers a great way to begin and maintain two-way conversations. The time commitment is minimal and users participating in the conversation are immediately identifiable. This method of lead generation can be utilized by any part of the sales process from any part of the organization, from individual sales persons to corporate marketing departments.

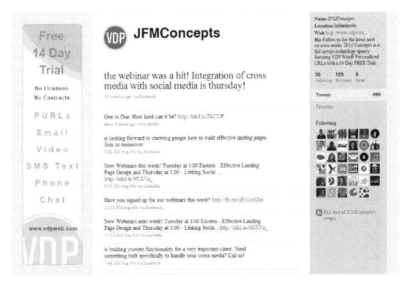

Be aware that there are real dangers to what company staff post online. In a well-documented internet blunder, a Vice President from Ketchum in Atlanta, a corporate communications firm, flew to a major clients' home city and made the following post to his Twitter account (@keyinfluencer) on the way to the meeting; "True confession but I'm in one of those towns where I scratch my head and say, 'I would die if I had to live here." This post was picked up by internal employees of the company who followed his account and the post was routed to the whole front office. Once published online, there is no way to pull a post off the web, even if the offending content is deleted. The same technology that allows both individuals and companies to reach the multitudes in seconds also means that mistakes are immediate and irreversible.

Tips for Social Media Quality Control

▸ Make sure that all corporate communications that may affect the brand are controlled. This includes employee accounts that are linked to the firm. Keep personal accounts and activities separate from business accounts unless the personal content is part of a carefully controlled brand strategy for lifestyle.

▸ Conduct common sense training on the use and dangers of social media and networking sites. Point out the obvious. Focus only on the positive or irrefutable when posting comments or blogging on any site.

▸ Write comments first and then come back to them later before posting if in doubt.

Cheating the System

Do not be tempted to cheat the system by adding fake reviews of products or services. The online paper trail is permanent and the fallout can be extreme. There have been several well documented instances of brand managers posting reviews themselves or paying for positive reviews. The damage they caused to the brand, and their employment longevity, is predictable.

It is common for firms to pay popular sites or authors to blog about a product or service. There are currently no Federal regulations that prohibit this activity, but United States government regulators are looking into potential conflicts of interest. It is best to use bloggers who disclose their financial relationships in order to avoid any kind of backlash.

COORDINATING SOCIAL MEDIA – HOOTSUITE

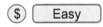

There are several social media coordination sites that allow users to make one entry and then have that content broadcast to numerous sites. This eliminates the need to log into every individual channel and cut and paste content. Many of these services, such as HootSuite, allow posts to be scheduled. This takes the burden off staff to manually execute a social media marketing plan. These types of tools are available as a software as a service at little to no cost, although some integrated tools are expensive.

TRACKING SOCIAL MEDIA MARKETING

Easy to use web tools make it possible to track how well your cross media efforts are doing at no charge. A very powerful tool is Google's free alert service, which will send notification emails to a subscriber when content is indexed. As the search engine finds the selected keywords and adds them to its database the alert email is triggered on a selected schedule. This is the easiest way to find when your organization or product appears in a blog post, release, commentary or other online location. Although web analytics are beyond the scope of this discussion, there are also ways to track web traffic and referrals in the web code. Some tools are free, at the cost of sharing your data with the provider, and others are available at many price points depending on the complexity of the information required.

As a final word of warning, be sure not to concentrate too much effort on any one channel or program. A change in the terms of service or popularity of any given tool could have immediate and lasting effect on a social media program. Keeping a diverse portfolio of content on the web will significantly mitigate this risk. Always be on the lookout for the next big thing. As buzz grows around a new outlet, consider its relevance to your strategy and decide when and if to add new channels and drop old ones.

Social Media: The Last Word

There are still many business leaders, including those in sales, marketing, and information technology that are mistakenly relegating Web 2.0's social media clout to teenagers and college

127

students. A 2007 study by Booz Allen Hamilton of 2,400 consumers in the United States, the United Kingdom and Germany concluded that companies that do not adjust their marketing and sales strategy to include social media are going to be at a disadvantage. These are a few interesting findings from the study:

▸ Cross media and Web 2.0 relevance cuts across gender and age. Forty-one percent of U.S. MySpace users are older than 35. The United Kingdom and Germany were thirty five and twenty nine percent respectively.

▸ Many Web 2.0 users have few privacy concerns. Sixty-four percent of U.S. messages are freely available to the public. U.K. respondents reported that number as 61 percent, while Germany reported 73 percent.

▸ Web 2.0 capitalizes on ubiquitous connectivity. Approximately one-quarter of surveyed MySpace users are accessing MySpace from a laptop, a school or office computer, an Internet-enabled cafe or a smart phone.

▸ Web 2.0 communities influence opinions and purchasing decisions. Thirty-nine percent of surveyed MySpace users receive product picks from virtual peers.

The study determines that the Internet is establishing itself more strongly in consumers' lives. In particular, Web 2.0-influenced trends will affect how businesses get and keep customers. The study lists opportunities that include shorter innovation cycles using customer integration, cross-media selling, customer service sites with end-user created content and wide participation, and using the internet as a brand channel. Web 2.0 is already at critical mass, the study concludes and businesses who don't respond are placing themselves at risk.

Advanced Web & Social Media Marketing 7

Advanced Web & Social Media Marketing

After a firm has been engaged in cross and social media marketing for a period of time it will become increasingly difficult to generate content. One way to overcome this challenge is to become involved with, or even to create, trade shows, conferences, speaking engagements and industry institutes. The following advanced web and social media marketing tools can be deployed to drive the firm and its content toward the hub of the conversation.

TRADE SHOWS, CONFERENCES & SPEAKING

 ⓢ ⓢ [Moderate]

Trade Shows and Conferences

Live events can offer incredible presence to a brand and provide a cross media marketing campaign material for all the other channels. Blogging, tweeting, and posting about the appearance and your organization's efforts is powerful content, especially if the appearance is not offered in exchange for sponsorship of the event.

The immediate response that many sales and marketing executives give is that exhibiting at trade shows and sponsoring conferences is too expensive. These events do involve large expenditures, but there are ways to capitalize on them without the overhead of a lavishly funded VC-backed start up or a Fortune 500 elephant.

By building a social media persona for both the firm and its key executives, companies can leverage that exposure into speaking engagements. Staff can act as subject matter experts at one of thousands of events specific to every vertical imaginable.

There are two ways to look at this category. The obvious one is to attend, exhibit, or advertise at a show sponsored by some other organization. The less obvious, and perhaps more powerful tool for many organizations, is to host a one or two day mini-event at a local facility and invite key clients and prospects. Vendors and channel partners, as well as outside industry experts, can be tapped to frame the conversation in a way the supports the host organization's strengths and agenda without being a hard sell. In addition to the direct sales opportunity, the social media content will extend far beyond the event itself.

Interface Series

Art Guild / Avalon hosts an annual one day event for key customers and suppliers in the trade show vertical. The event is a mini trade show for non-competitive vendors to provide a forum for new ideas and content that can be accessed at a highly personal level. The scheduled speakers have no commercial interest in the proceedings and the there is real value imparted to the invited guests. The result for the host firm is a boost to the ongoing relationship with existing customers and vendors and a treasure trove of content for cross media applications.

Speaking Engagements

By using social media to become a recognized industry expert, opportunities will arise for sales and marketing leaders to present at various events. These engagements can come at no cost to the organization and further position the firm's leaders as objective subject matter experts. The appearance can be leveraged by the firm in a wide variety of corporate communications from social media to press releases. The quality of contacts that can be generated on site while walking the floor with a "Speaker" ribbon attached to your credentials is worth the effort. One more tip: Be sure to talk up your sessions as you work the event to assure good attendance.

There is no need to spend a small fortune to participate in industry events. Start at a local or regional level, build credibility and a good story, and the business benefits will follow. The media and marketing coverage from the event can be leveraged to provide a springboard of marketing content for attending firms at a fraction of the cost of attending large shows as a sponsor or exhibitor.

INDUSTRY COVERAGE

Many web venues for news media are dominated by industry sites that accept advertising and give preference to large corporations and their main advertisers over small firms. Involvement, often in the way of paid advertising, is the best way to be covered by industry news and media outlets. Those firms that sponsor various web and live events, pay for banner ads, and exhibit at the outlet's various shows will find that they receive extensive coverage in the "news" section of the website, blog, or industry trade publication in question. In many cases, these firms engage with associations and trade or industry groups in a marketing quid pro quo. The cost of this type of media and market group coverage may be high, but it may also offer direct and immediate access to a channel that focuses on the firm's core universe of prospects. That being said, it is possible to build a reputation as a subject matter expert in order to overcome this obstacle.

INDUSTRY INSTITUTE

The ultimate web marketing platform is to create an independently branded industry information site that presents itself like a trade organization. The main goal is to help the marketing and sales manager guide the conversation across the industry in ways that support the firm's strengths and agenda. Manufacturers and software firms can leverage user groups as part of this program. Companies that support products from different manufacturers can make user groups and forums for each product line.

Experts for content and support are easy to find as they get a chance to build their professional reputations and soft sell their products and services. Recognition as industry experts is a key benefit that will get the Institute content generated for free. These institutes can begin primarily as web based entities and then expand into a live operation with conferences and other events.

An industry institute web site can be built using online templates for minimal cost and should include most of the following elements:

▸ RSS feed of industry news content

▸ Schedule of institute supported training classes, events and webinars

▸ Contact form and institute phone number or email

▸ Links to institute specific social media pages

▸ Speaker's bureau

▸ Book store and call for books to publish

▸ Advertising (including the sponsor's brand and non-competitive industry players)

▸ Expert advice column – "ask the experts" with the staff supported by non-competing or friendly industry persons

Example Institute

SeaSecure, a maritime security firm in Fort Lauderdale, Florida which has subsequently been sold to TransSystems, built a profitable client base in large part by creating the Maritime Security Institute. The Institute had its own web site, newsletter, blog, training classes and content which provided legitimacy to the training provided by the sponsoring firm. The security classes offered by the Institute were executed by SeaSecure. Training was a core competency and major revenue driver for the host company. The main sales vehicle for the training sessions was the Institute. In this way, the Maritime Security Institute, a not for profit organization, could advertise training as a non-biased service and earn the trust of attendees.

Industry Conferences

The Institute can be leveraged to include an industry trade show that specifically targets the information, concerns, and issues that the firm is best able to address and that the company's products or services can support. A series of small one or two day events in regional cities can be launched with moderate expense and risk in conjunction with all of the other web marketing efforts of the firm. This is a particularly powerful approach for any firm that has a significant consultation arm to their business.

Although the creation and launch of an industry institute is a major undertaking, it is certainly an achievable goal. The man hours and resources required may be less than a major marketing effort. For small businesses at the larger end of the scale, mid-sized, and large business, this option has great potential.

Implementation *8*

Implementation

It should be clear by this point that the goal of cross media marketing is to gain as wide of an audience as possible across as many channels as possible. The most important implementation step for a cross media plan is the recognition that not only is a social media presence a pre-requisite for success in the modern business world, but that it is also an achievable objective. The integration of additional channels to the existing marketing mix can be immediately incorporated and at minimal cost. As an outline of where to begin, the following basic plans are laid out in terms of effort and budget.

Low Effort & Budget

▸ Company and Key Executive LinkedIn, Facebook, and Twitter accounts with links to content

▸ Links on landing pages, company website and social media sites to press releases

▸ Occasional contribution to content in industry trade group blogs & forums

▸ Quarterly newsletter

▸ Opt-in form on landing pages

▸ Small budget paid search with one landing page

Medium Effort & Budget

▸ All of the above, plus:

▸ Company blog with weekly posts

▸ Monthly newsletter

▸ Membership in industry trade groups

▸ Paid search with content specific landing pages

▸ Improve naturalized search engine optimization

All-Out Blitz & Budget

▸ All of the above, plus:

▸ Create an industry institute or join leadership in one

▸ Institute trade show and/or seminar series

▸ Company blog with daily content

▸ Frequent content submissions to industry trade groups and forums

▸ Extensive paid search with ad specific landing pages

▸ Sponsorship of events and trade shows

The low effort and budget plan may not seem like an extraordinary amount of work, but these suggestions make the assumption that most organizations will be pursing cross media efforts without the benefit of additional resources. In the fortuitous event that budget and staff are available, then much more can be accomplished.

WHEN SALES ARE SLOW

Many firms are slow during particular seasons or because of the economy and they are taking the opportunity to relax. A better idea is to take staff and management time during this lull to revamp web sites, create new content, and get involved in social media. The investment in brand and content can be leveraged across multiple channels to capture additional sales and make the case for the company's value proposition as strong as possible.

Review & Revise Strategic Plans

When was the last time the business and marketing plan was cracked open from those dusty binders on the bookshelf? More importantly, when was the last time the leadership team got together to systematically discuss strategic marketing and sales issues? For most firms the answer is rarely or never. Time may be limited, but a review of plans against current operations may point our weaknesses or deficiencies that have been overlooked. Resources can be dedicated during down time to address any issues that are discovered.

Blog, Tweet and Get LinkedIn

I was almost certainly the last owner of a tech firm to break down and get a smart phone. For a long time the entire concept of social media seemed silly and not a real business activity. At

some point in the last three years press releases stopped perform-
ing unless it was picked up by a well-read blog and I started to
see the light. After a recent sales call, the first thing the prospect
did was look me up on LinkedIn and then he spent time reading
my blog before he agreed to a meeting. The prospect never even
went to our corporate website. Social media exposure only costs
time and if business is slow, there is an opportunity to jump start
a program.

Update Paid Search

If your firm is anything like the average, paid search is like a
Ronco Rotisserie; "Set it and forget it." Running large paid
search campaigns effectively can rapidly become a full time job.
In the face of pressing matters, doing more than checking a
few reports seems onerous. Slow periods are the perfect time
to double check keywords, revamp ad copy, and freshen the
campaign.

Review Search Engine Optimization

There are lots of checklists and procedures floating around the
web on how to improve naturalized search position on Google
and the other search engines. There are all kinds of tests that can
be performed and small, cost effective steps that can be taken
to improve how the site is indexed. Downtime is the perfect
opportunity to dedicate resources to a search engine optimization project which can passively support the sales cycle 24/7.

Add Fresh Content

As a part of search engine optimization and as a standalone sales tool, update and add content to the company website and blog. The major search engines love updated content. Consider creating specialized landing pages that highlight company strengths and integrate those pages with social media and paid search efforts for key strategic business lines. This is easy to do even if web work is outsourced or the IT guys are hard to get along with.

Content can include:

- Articles
- Tech Tips
- Blog Posts
- How to Guides
- Videos
- Case Studies
- Tutorials
- Product Notes

Reach Out to the Prospect List & Clients with a Newsletter

When was the last time something was sent to clients and prospects without a direct sales pitch? Since the time has been spent to create new content for social media, search engine optimization (SEO), and the website, it is ready for direct communication to house file contacts. If business is slow, chances are customers and prospects are slow too. Use the time wisely.

EXECUTING A SOCIAL MEDIA MARKETING STRATEGY

Sharing makes a firm interesting. Promote content to the company's network to create a wide reach with the following four steps.

1. Build The Network

▸ Interact with popular people, sites & blogs

▸ Answer questions – most social media sites have forums and discussions

▸ Provide links to content from the company's social media accounts

2. Publish Valuable Information

New market data, educational content, and other relevant posts are more likely to be shared than product info, free trials, documentation, and hard sales pitches.

Create a blog and update it regularly with fresh content. Topics can include:

▸ Webcasts

▸ Videos

▸ Photos & Samples

▸ Presentations

▸ News Releases

145

- Case Studies

- Practical Guides

- Links to relevant content

- Product and features announcements

3. Reach Out to Followers

Track who interacts with the firm and reach out to them, even if they do not reach out to you. Prospects do not need to raise their hand to be identified as warm leads. If they follow you and your content, you need to contact them directly.

Do not let the lack of an automated system prevent follow up from occurring in a timely fashion. Marketing automation would be nice to have, but it can be expensive and difficult to implement. Most small to midsize businesses do not have the budget for custom developed marketing systems. The price point of these systems is dropping every year. Many firms offer trickle marketing in both print and email from data pulled from CRM systems.

4. Measure & React

How are you converting leads into sales? Whether you are in sales or marketing, justifying ROI is critical. Determine which channels are providing the most leads and highest conversion rates and then concentrate resources in these areas.

And when things finally pick up? Keep at it, five minutes a day.

TOP CROSS MEDIA IMPLEMENTATION ERRORS

The following list details the most common errors in the implementation of cross media marketing programs.

✔ Not taking the first steps

It may be daunting to coordinate marketing efforts across channels. In small firms there is not enough time and in large ones politics and cross departmental coordination makes any task difficult. The opportunity cost of not making this effort a priority is so high that not starting is not an option.

✔ Not considering marketing efforts across channels

Most marketers overlook the fact that every campaign can be coordinated with minimal effort and without a major overhaul to existing efforts. Use unique phone numbers, web addresses and landing pages to track results and collect all the response metrics in one place. A simple spreadsheet will do if there is no better option or the budget is not available for a more sophisticated solution. Managers with different areas of responsibility must be forced to coordinate their efforts across all product lines and channels. Every touch is valuable and too expensive to waste.

✔ Relying on one channel

In many cases marketers tend to focus on one or two channels. Even sophisticated organizations which utilize a broad spectrum of media tend to focus their efforts on a few favorites. It is well established that customers are more likely to buy in their preferred channel if they have been touched by another. Direct mail drives internet sales and websites drive brick and mortar purchases. Coordinating channels, and putting a mechanism in place to allow customers to let their references be known, will dramatically improve marketing effectiveness.

✔ Using a weak web address

Some firms will use a special web page on their main site, like www.acme.com/offer to try and track a specific offer but the "/offer" is often truncated by the respondent. By changing the web address to www.acmeoffers.com, relevant content is always served. This is especially true of broadcast media where the link is not in front of the user.

✔ Ignoring the power of the landing page

What radio, TV, print, direct mail or email advertisement today does not include a web address? From NPR, to Field & Stream, to the internet, copywriters casually throw in the company website as a response channel. There is no way to tell if the traffic came from search engine optimization, paid search, or a printed piece. Additionally, the content seen by visitor is not specific to the advertisement that drove them to the site in the first place.

More than coordinating across channels is important to successful marketing campaigns. Customers must be effectively engaged. By actively soliciting their input and preferences marketers can maximize the return of every marketing dollar spent. Specific landing pages accomplish that at very low cost.

✔ Controlling the conversation

Today's marketer, more than ever, must let the customer control the marketing conversation. By letting the responder choose the channels and content, relevancy will increase and response rates and ROI will follow. This choice can be active or passive. Tracking links on a page is a passive technique while asking a question is an active one.

✔ Not creating two-way communications & asking questions

Customers will answer almost any question they are asked. By simply giving the opportunity to easily provide input the quantity and quality of data collected can be staggering. Most customers need a good reason to provide an email or phone number, but they will answer preference questions without hesitation. By using personalization across various media we can identify these prospects and assign the feedback to their customer record.

✔ Not implementing data collection mechanisms

 Every contact is an opportunity to learn more about the customer. Always have link tracking, opt-in, quick surveys, and other feedback mechanisms on every touch made in order to increase your market intelligence. The web makes this type of data collection easy to execute. Even if the response rates are low, by systemically leveraging every touch, the results can be dramatic.

✔ Creating data silos

Assure that internet, CRM, trade show, direct mail, email, SMS Text, social media, broadcast, point of sale, and phone contacts ultimately feed into one database. Even if this process must be done manually, data is data and can be combined. Virtually every system in use has an export feature and managers at every level must make this collection a top priority.

Driving customers to the web and presenting the opportunity to provide input is the first step in creating sophisticated cross channel campaigns. There can be no excuse for not beginning to coordinate marketing efforts, even if the first step is as simple as creating a new landing page that each channel in a project uses to collect data. Even small efforts will rapidly build a powerful house file of warm leads that will provide the best source of revenue.

Conclusion 9

Conclusion

The future of cross media marketing is wide open and will continue to change as technology develops and the general population becomes more used to communicating electronically. The applications and channels in vogue may come and go, but a few things are certain. There will be more channels for marketers to contend with every year, not less. The markets in all channels will continue to specialize and splinter as the promulgation of content becomes easier as entities with little to no capital produce and distribute on an international scale.

Mobile phones and tablet devices that provide instantaneous connectivity to the internet continue to add functionality, usefulness, and fall in cost. As user interfaces improve, increasing reliance will be placed on this channel for both business and consumer activity.

WHAT SHOULD I DO RIGHT NOW?

As marketing or sales leader, the immediate task at hand is to maximize the returns on current efforts. The principle considerations when reviewing the existing marketing mix for any size firm include:

▸ Conduct a complete review of the entire marketing mix and begin to question the return generated by each channel

▸ Utilize as many collection mechanisms as practical in every marketing contact

152

▸ Assure that every reasonable effort is made to collect and consolidate data from all channels in the current media mix

▸ Engage both customers and prospects in two-way conversations via cross media on every touch

▸ Verify that contact preferences and opt-ins are presented at every opportunity

▸ Assure that follow up activities are developed, documented and executed for each channel

If certain campaigns have been committed to either contractually, as part of the corporate culture or are otherwise beyond reconsideration, make sure to do the following:

▸ Utilize a unique phone number to track responses in place of the main sales number

▸ Add landing pages specific to the campaign in place of a generic web address on all channels

▸ Establish a baseline result from existing efforts and test against that channel by testing

▸ Introduce new response mechanisms such as SMS Text to statistically significant portions of the current marketing

It is necessary to act decisively to improve tracking and measurement of efforts across the marketing mix. The insight to be gained by using accurate metrics to assign relative value to the different channels employed will help sales and marketing leaders make the best choices possible in the allocation of scarce resources. In many cases, being able to defend the budgetary decisions made and to show how those decisions were measured may not only make the next budgetary cycle go more smoothly, but may also save your job. Even if the reporting shows that a particular effort did not perform as expected, the executive can point this out the plan to overcome the deficiency by shifting to channels with better return.

The key is to show a consistent and thought out plan for deploying scarce resources. Staffing levels and resources are unlikely to rise, and for most marketing and sales departments will continue to fall. By moving the needle each quarter, sales and marketing leadership can maintain better control of their fate.

Appendix

Appendix A: Cross Media Campaign

The following cross media campaign is included as a real world example to show the flexibility of cross media applications. Although it features a large multi-national, the decision makers and budget came from front line managers who did not have access to corporate IT or Marketing support.

HEWLETT PACKARD

HP is the world's largest IT company. Despite impressive marketing expenditures, it is often challenging for product and channel managers to access enterprise resources to conduct integrated marketing efforts. The goals of this campaign were to:

▸ Generate qualified leads for both the company and value added reseller sales representatives.

▸ Effectively touch multiple HP channels, products, and brands across broad geographic territories.

▸ Provide hundreds of relevant offers, content, and copy for various partners and business units with minimal effort from managers and little or no corporate marketing or IT support.

SOLUTION

A software as a service (SasS) was chosen as the cross media platform on which a multitiered effort utilizing variable data direct mail, email, static print, and landing page URLs printed in various publications was built. Content was based on existing HP collaterals to minimize production costs, time to market, and legal review. Offers and terms were recycled from existing efforts to assure that minimal support would be required from corporate resources.

The unified campaign was designed to either drive response by unique 800 number or web visit. Actions taken by the prospect online were recorded and scored. Sales leads were instantly sent to all interested parties and automatic follow up was conducted based on business logic and scheduled touch points.

DIRECT MAIL

The direct mail component of the campaign featured variable data postcards. Recipients were segmented by reseller partner and channel as required. Responders could call the reseller or

HP directly using various unique 800 numbers as appropriate or they could visit their personalized landing page. Visitors were tracked with "seed" content that was designed to both educate and demonstrate a level of interest based on product lines.

EMAIL

A significant part of the campaign featured email. There were dozens of iterations based on vertical and channel. A simple spreadsheet was created to define the business logic and marketing plan. This information was used to create an ongoing lead generation and nurturing program which segmented recipients into responders and non-responders. Each group was then filtered into the appropriate communications strategy. Responders were polled to determine their preferred communications channel.

STATIC PRINT & ADVERTISING

Generic URLs featuring offer-specific content were used in place of the corporate hp.com website. This allowed individual brand managers and resellers to add content to the web without access to corporate IT support. Additionally, stakeholders had instant access to reporting metrics without having to rely on headquarters to disseminate information.

LANDING PAGES

HP utilized multiple designs, styles, and formats of micro sites with variable links, text, video, and reseller logos for each campaign. Sites ranged from one to seven pages depending on the content and marketing purpose. These sites included:

Personal Information Portals

The most powerful microsites featured a video spokesperson and tracked links that were used to "score" prospects based on what information they downloaded or viewed. Content included video, whitepapers, and case studies.

Unsolicited Proposals

Based on a firm's business type and size, HP sent out unsolicited proposals that were customized to the client's demographics.

Informational Pages

Single landing pages featuring specific product lines, services, or promotions were created to measure response by advertising channel.

TARGET AUDIENCE AND MESSAGING

There were multiple target audiences for this campaign depending on the business unit of HP or the reseller group that was being supported. Campaigns were run for such diverse product lines and channels as cloud computing, virtualization, wide format printing, networking and more. Content was data driven to minimize production time while at the same time creating a robust and personalized message to each recipient.

DATA

Contacts were gathered from a variety of sources in a coordinated effort to eliminate data silos and assign unique identifiers that could be matched back across various platforms. The goal was to standardize diverse data schemas. Channel partner and HP contacts were merged into a single data file that could be segmented, tracked, and analyzed to identify broad patterns.

CREATIVE AND OUTBOUND PIECES

The creative for the outbound piece was drawn from existing collaterals to minimize copy writing, review and design time. The postcard designs were intentionally kept simple to capture the recipients attention in the "mail moment."

RESULTS

For the first time, HP and reseller managers without access to corporate marketing support were able to deploy complex variable data campaigns. Cold sales lists produced consistent responses in the 4 to 6% range while highly segmented offers to warm leads scored 30% or higher. Respondents were further segmented based on their online actions in response to both email and direct mail solicitations.

REASONS FOR SUCCESS

The key factor for the success of this complex multichannel, multi-business unit campaign was the ability to provide turn key service. Business unit managers and value added reseller partners were not required to contribute materially to the process. Individual marketers were able to coordinate the entire effort without enterprise level support. Long deployment and development times were avoided by providing all stakeholders a minimal workload and a central point of contact for all campaign requirements including content, design, data, and deployment. By providing tracking across multiple channels in one dashboard, it was easy for managers to see the relative value of their marketing spend and ensure that they were appropriately distributing their budgets. Data collection was also added to all channels in the marketing mix without a change in strategy being required.

BEST PRACTICES FROM CAMPAIGN

▸ Minimize the effort required of the client / manager to provide content and creative – leverage existing materials and website information for offers and design.

▸ Use PURLs to track responses on all variable channels.

▸ Use Generic URLs, or static landing pages, to track results from static collaterals.

▸ Communicate with prospects multiple times and on multiple channels to start a two-way conversation and determine needs.

Appendix B: Email Marketing Rules

CAN-SPAM ACT

Requirements for Commercial Emailers

The CAN-SPAM Act of 2003 (Controlling the Assault of Non-Solicited Pornography and Marketing Act) establishes requirements for those who send commercial email, spells out penalties for spammers and companies whose products are advertised in spam if they violate the law, and gives consumers the right to ask emailers to stop spamming them.

The law, which became effective January 1, 2004, covers email whose primary purpose is advertising or promoting a commercial product or service, including content on a Web site. A "transactional or relationship message" – email that facilitates an agreed-upon transaction or updates a customer in an existing business relationship – may not contain false or misleading routing information, but otherwise is exempt from most provisions of the CAN-SPAM Act.

The Federal Trade Commission (FTC), the nation's consumer protection agency, is authorized to enforce the CAN-SPAM Act. CAN-SPAM also gives the Department of Justice (DOJ) the authority to enforce its criminal sanctions. Other federal and state agencies can enforce the law against organizations under their jurisdiction, and companies that provide Internet access may sue violators, as well.

163

WHAT THE LAW REQUIRES

Here's a rundown of the law's main provisions:

▸ It bans false or misleading header information. Your email's "From," "To," and routing information – including the originating domain name and email address – must be accurate and identify the person who initiated the email.

▸ It prohibits deceptive subject lines. The subject line cannot mislead the recipient about the contents or subject matter of the message.

▸ It requires that your email give recipients an opt-out method. You must provide a return email address or another Internet-based response mechanism that allows a recipient to ask you not to send future email messages to that email address, and you must honor the requests. You may create a "menu" of choices to allow a recipient to opt out of certain types of messages, but you must include the option to end any commercial messages from the sender.

▸ Any opt-out mechanism you offer must be able to process opt-out requests for at least 30 days after you send your commercial email. When you receive an opt-out request, the law gives you 10 business days to stop sending email to the requestor's email address. You cannot help another entity send email to that address, or have another entity send email on your behalf to that address. Finally, it's illegal for you to sell or transfer the email addresses of people who choose not to receive your email, even in the form of a mailing list, unless you transfer the addresses so another entity can comply with the law.

▶ It requires that commercial email be identified as an advertisement and include the sender's valid physical postal address. Your message must contain clear and conspicuous notice that the message is an advertisement or solicitation and that the recipient can opt out of receiving more commercial email from you. It also must include your valid physical postal address.

PENALTIES

Each violation of the above provisions is subject to fines of up to $16,000. Deceptive commercial email also is subject to laws banning false or misleading advertising.

Additional fines are provided for commercial emailers who not only violate the rules described above, but also:

▶ "Harvest" email addresses from Web sites or Web services that have published a notice prohibiting the transfer of email addresses for the purpose of sending email

▶ Generate email addresses using a "dictionary attack" – combining names, letters, or numbers into multiple permutations

▶ Use scripts or other automated ways to register for multiple email or user accounts to send commercial email

▸ Relay emails through a computer or network without permission – for example, by taking advantage of open relays or open proxies without authorization.

The law allows the DOJ to seek criminal penalties, including imprisonment, for commercial emailers who do – or conspire to:

▸ Use another computer without authorization and send commercial email from or through it

▸ Use a computer to relay or retransmit multiple commercial email messages to deceive or mislead recipients or an Internet access service about the origin of the message

▸ Falsify header information in multiple email messages and initiate the transmission of such messages

▸ Register for multiple email accounts or domain names using information that falsifies the identity of the actual registrant

▸ Falsely represent themselves as owners of multiple Internet Protocol addresses that are used to send commercial email messages.

ADDITIONAL RULES

The FTC will issue additional rules under the CAN-SPAM Act involving the required labeling of sexually explicit commercial email and the criteria for determining "the primary purpose" of a commercial email.

Look for the rule covering the labeling of sexually explicit material in April 2004; "the primary purpose" rulemaking will be complete by the end of 2004. The Act also instructs the FTC to report to Congress in summer 2004 on a National Do Not E-Mail Registry, and issue reports in the next two years on the labeling of all commercial email, the creation of a "bounty system" to promote enforcement of the law, and the effectiveness and enforcement of the CAN-SPAM Act.

See the FTC Web site at www.ftc.gov/spam for updates on implementation of the CAN-SPAM Act.

The FTC maintains a consumer complaint database of violations of the laws that the FTC enforces. Consumers can submit complaints online at www.ftc.gov and forward unwanted commercial email to the FTC at spam@uce.gov.

FOR MORE INFORMATION

The FTC works for the consumer to prevent fraudulent, deceptive, and unfair practices in the marketplace and to provide information to businesses to help them comply with the law. To file a complaint or to get free information on consumer issues, visit ftc.gov or call toll-free, 1-877-FTC-HELP (1-877-382-4357); TTY: 1-866-653-4261. The FTC enters Internet, telemarketing, identity theft, and other fraud-related complaints into Consumer Sentinel, a secure online database available to hundreds of civil and criminal law enforcement agencies in the U.S. and abroad.

Source: *Federal Trade Commission*

Appendix C: Resources

EMAIL MARKETING

Federal Trade Commission Email Summary

http://business.ftc.gov/documents/bus61-can-spam-act-compliance-guide-business

MOBILE MARKETING / SMS TEXT

Common Short Code Administration (CSCA)

http://www.usshortcodes.com

Mobile Marketing Association

http://www.mmaglobal.com

Best Practices Guidelines

http://mmaglobal.com/bestpractices.pdf

The Wireless Association (CITA)

http://www.ctia.org

SOCIAL MEDIA MARKETING

Facebook Marketing Bible

http://www.insidefacebook.com/facebook-marketing-bible/

REAL TIME PERSONALIZATION

Profile Complete

http://www.profilecomplete.com

CROSS MEDIA MARKETING PLATFORM / SERVICES

VDP Web

http://www.vdpweb.com

VDP Complete

http://www.vdpcomplete.com

SITEMAPS

http://www.xml-sitemaps.com

Shameless Plug

Consulting & Speaking

James D. Michelson is an engaging speaker with a highly personal and energetic style that engages the audience and invites them into the session. Audiences feel they are active participants and become truly engaged to the content presented. James adjusts each keynote, presentation, or session to the needs of the audience and makes changes on the fly based on both his perception of the audience and their feedback. The level of detail can be tailored to the needs of the event from strategic overviews to practical, hands on applications.

POPULAR TOPICS INCLUDE

▸ Linking Social and Cross Media Marketing

▸ Cross Media Marketing Outlook

▸ Tactics to Make Marketers Excel in the C-Suite

▸ A Practical Guide to Generating Leads from Social Media

▸ Increasing Revenue - Keep More of your Customer's Marketing Budget

▸ Using & Reusing Intelligent Content for 1:1 Cross Media Marketing

▸ Surviving as the CMO in the New Age

▸ Surviving as a Sales Executive in the New Age

▶ Creating Programs That Generate and Measure ROI from Specific Marketing Channels

▶ Adding New Media Channels to the Marketing Mix

RECENT AUDIENCES

▶ Marketing Service Providers & Agencies

▶ Commercial Printers and Mailers

▶ Not for Profits

▶ Membership Organizations

▶ Direct Marketers

▶ Trade Show Vendors, Exhibitors and Producers

Visit **www.jmichelson.com** for more information.

Cross Media Marketing

VDP Web® is a software as a service that provides the best value and functionality without long term contracts.

VDP Web combines PURLs, Email, SMS Text, QR Codes, Variable Video, Video Spokesmen, 800# Tracking, Generic Landing Pages (GURLs), and more in one platform that avoids data silos and can tie into any CRM. Explore all the possibilities at **www.vdpweb.com**.

Hundreds of firms have trusted VDP Complete® to execute world class cross media campaigns. Award winning campaigns from JFM Concepts produce measurable returns and provide detailed tracking and reporting. Learn more at **www.vdpcomplete.com**.

Profile Complete® identifies callers or visitors to a website and appends demographic information to the specific visitor in real time utilizing data from national sources. The web visitor is then provided personalized content based on their persona to maximize engagement and dramatically improve ROI. Visit **www.profilecomplete.com** for more information.

For more information, call 800-735-2578.

11854689R0010

Made in the USA
Lexington, KY
05 November 2011